Tax Guid   SA

C

WINNING
YOUR
AUDIT

by

Holmes F. Crouch
Tax Specialist

Published by

Allyear Tax Guides

**20484 Glen Brae Drive
Saratoga, CA 95070**

ISBN 0-944817-46-7

LCCN 97-75300

Printed in U.S.A.

Series 500
Audits and Appeals

Tax Guide 502

WINNING YOUR AUDIT

For other titles in print, see page 224.

The author: **Holmes F. Crouch**
For more about the author, see page 221.

PREFACE

If you are a knowledge-seeking **taxpayer** looking for information, this book can be helpful to you. It is designed to be read — from cover to cover — in less than eight hours. Or, it can be "skim-read" in about 30 minutes.

Either way, you are treated to **tax knowledge** . . . *beyond the ordinary*. The "beyond" is that which cannot be found in IRS publications, FedWorld on-line services, tax software programs, or on CD-ROMs.

Taxpayers have different levels of interest in a selected subject. For this reason, this book starts with introductory fundamentals and progresses onward. You can verify the progression by chapter and section in the table of contents. In the text, "applicable law" is quoted in pertinent part. Key phrases and key tax forms are emphasized. Real-life examples are given . . . in down-to-earth style.

This book has 12 chapters. This number provides depth without cross-subject rambling. Each chapter starts with a head summary of meaningful information.

To aid in your skim-reading, informative diagrams and tables are placed strategically throughout the text. By leafing through page by page, reading the summaries and section headings, and glancing at the diagrams and tables, you can get a good handle on the matters covered.

Effort has been made to update and incorporate all of the latest tax law changes that are *significant* to the title subject. However, "beyond the ordinary" does not encompass every conceivable variant of fact and law that might give rise to protracted dispute and litigation. Consequently, if a particular statement or paragraph is crucial to your own specific case, you are urged to seek professional counseling. Otherwise, the information presented is general and is designed for a broad range of reader interests.

The Author

INTRODUCTION

You arrive home from work one day, and pick up your mail. There's an envelope from:

Department of the Treasury
Internal Revenue Service

Thinking it's another tax refund you open the envelope with pleased anticipation. You unfold several sheets of paper and begin looking at the first sheet. You cannot find where it begins. There's no salutation of any kind. In the upper right-hand corner there is a preprinted directive: **Person to Contact**, followed by a telephone number. This makes no sense to you at all.

You see a stick-on label with 15 digits stretched across it. Immediately below these numbers, your name appears. Below your name is some white space, followed by your address. You recognize your zip code. Then there is more white space.

You now begin to read what is obviously a bureaucratic form letter. It says—

Your Federal income tax return has been selected for examination. On the reverse side please see the specific items for the tax year(s) shown below. **It is very important that you contact our office within 10 days from the date of this letter** *. . . to arrange an appointment. For your convenience, the following space is provided to record the appointment:*

Or, out of the blue, you may receive a phone call. The caller will say (or words similar):

This is Mr./Ms. _____ of the Internal Revenue Service. Your Federal tax returns for the year(s) _____ have been assigned to me for examination. I've set up an appointment for you on _____ (date) _____ , for the examination to be conducted at your place of business, your home, or other designated place. If this is satisfactory, I'll send you a confirming letter to this effect.

You're taken aback by the caller, so you stutter and stumble. Or, you are puzzled by the "letter" you received. Then the light strikes.

"Oh, good grief!" you exclaim. "I'm being audited. Why me? I pay my taxes. I pay *their* salaries, *their* pensions, *their* vacation fun, and *their* medical benefits. What more do they want?"

Your hands begin to tremble. Anger and frustration begin to boil from within. Your blood pressure is up. Your head begins to throb. Your eyes become blurry. You look at the bureaucratic form letter, but you can't read any more. Then you spot the attachments.

"What are all these attachments for?" you say. "Can't they tell me in simple language what they want?"

No. They can't tell you what they want. Because they don't really know themselves. They are seine fishing in taxpayer waters. They want more tax revenue, but they can't come out and demand it until *after* they have examined your return.

So, what do you do?

We will tell you what to do throughout this book. Much depends on the type of information on your return. We will tell you how to win your audit, and prosper by the experience.

You *can* win your audit. Yes, you can. Approximately 30% of all auditees do win.

In the meantime, you should know that you are one of about 3,000,000 (3 million) taxpayers who receive audit "letters" each year. Ordinarily, you have not been picked out for special prosecution or for government harassment. You are simply part of Big Brother's computer selection process designed to wring more money from docile citizenry.

Of those returns selected for audit, approximately 70% wind up paying additional taxes. On the average nationwide, each auditee pays about $2,560 in additional money. This nets the government an additional $7,680,000,000 (7.68 *billion*) in revenue annually. Still, this is not enough to defray federal pay raises, congressional salaries, judicial pensions, and executive branch vacations.

So, it is up to you. Do you want to be among the 70% auditees who pay additionally into the federal trough? Or, do you want to be among the 30% winners?

If the latter, then you should read on.

CONTENTS

1

PURPOSE(S) OF AUDIT

The Ordinary Purpose Of An Audit Is To Ascertain The "Correct Tax." In The Process, There Is Probability That Additional Revenue Will Accrue To Government. The Statutory Authority For Tax Audits Is Embodied In Section 7602. It Is Enforceable By Summons. This "Power To Audit" Is Awesome . . . And Often Abusive. Other Purposes Involve Lifestyle Probing, "Cover" For Other Agencies, Training Of Personnel, Compliance Measurements (Research), Public Imaging, Surveillance of Payees, And Pyramiding Of Penalties . . . For Still More Revenue.

The term "audit" means to examine a specific item of account with intent to verify its accuracy. It also means the establishment of proof via a trail of documentation prepared by third-party interests.

A "third-party" is someone, or some entity, *other* than the taxpayer being audited and *other* than the government agent doing the audit. The taxpayer has a biased interest in minimizing his taxes; the government has a biased interest in maximizing tax revenues. A true third-party interest, therefore, is biased in neither direction. It identifies the facts and circumstances as they actually occur.

Thus, an objective and proper audit can work as much against the government as for it. Similarly, an audit can work as much *for* the taxpayer as against him . . . or her.

Unfortunately, the term "audit" has a stigma associated with it. It implies some sort of wrongdoing by the person being audited.

This is *not* the case at all. Too much adverse publicity concerning tax audits has broadcast this unjust implication.

Although there may be some improper deduction or expense claimed on a tax return, the government has no foreknowledge of this. One's selection for audit is primarily a mechanical (computer) processing matter. The government ostensibly is looking for more revenue. For this, it programs its computers to flag those returns which indicate a *probability* of producing additional revenue.

Code Section 7602

The first internal revenue laws were formulated in 1913. They derive directly from Amendment 16 of the U.S. Constitution. This now-famous amendment reads in full as follows—

The Congress shall have power to lay and collect taxes on income, from whatever source derived, without apportionment among the several states, and without regard to any census or enumeration.

Note that there are just 30 words to this all-powerful consititutional amendment.

Note also that "Congress shall have the power to . . . ." This power to tax is not in the hands of federal judges, nor federal agencies, nor the Internal Revenue Service, nor the President himself. The power to tax is in the lap of Congress.

Congress, therefore, is the enacting body which approves or disapproves all tax laws. Members of Congress — the House and Senate — are elected by a simple majority of those citizens who are eligible to vote. This supposedly means that what Congress does, the public approves. We may quarrel with this thesis, but it is the premise upon which our tax laws are based.

So much for constitutional background. Where do we find the specific statutory basis for the Internal Revenue Service to conduct tax audits at will?

Answer: Section 7602 of the Internal Revenue Code. This "Code" is a 2,500,000-word (2.5 million) body of tax law enacted by Congress over the years since 1913.

Section 7602 is captioned: *Examination of Books and Witnesses.* Its subsection (a) reads in full as follows—

For the purpose of ascertaining the correctness of any return, making a return where none has been made, determining the liability of any person for any internal revenue tax or the liability at law or in equity of any transferee or fiduciary of any person in respect of any internal revenue tax, or collecting any such liability, the Secretary is authorized—
(1) To examine any books, papers, records or other data which may be relevant or material to such inquiry;
(2) To summon the person liable for tax or required to perform the act, or any officer or employee of such person, or any person having possession, custody, or care of books of account containing entries relating to the business of the person liable for tax or required to perform the act, or any other person the Secretary may deem proper, to appear before the Secretary at a time and place named in the summons and to produce such books, papers, records, or other data, and to give such testimony, under oath, as may be relevant or material to such inquiry.

There are about 180 words in Section 7602(a). There are approximately 1,800 tax code sections, some longer and some shorter than Section 7602. They all derive from the 30 words of Amendment 16!

The term "Secretary" (in Section 7602) means the Secretary of the Treasury *or his delegate*. The term "or his delegate" means any officer, employee, or agency of the U.S. Treasury Department. One such agency is the Internal Revenue Service (IRS). There are other agencies of the Treasury Department as depicted in Figure 1.1.

Note that we show in Figure 1.1 the IRS as a separate, detached agency from all others in the Treasury Department. We show it this way purposely because the IRS, indeed, behaves as a separate "government" unto itself.

The IRS acts differently from other government agencies because the wording in Section 7602 is not well publicized. Every auditee, therefore, should be aware of Section 7602. He need not be familiar with its every word, but he should know that the proper statutory authority does exist. Any feeling that a tax audit is "unconstitutional" has no standing. If you dare resist on constitutional grounds, you are tagged by the IRS as a "tax protester." Then, unconscionable penalties are assessed.

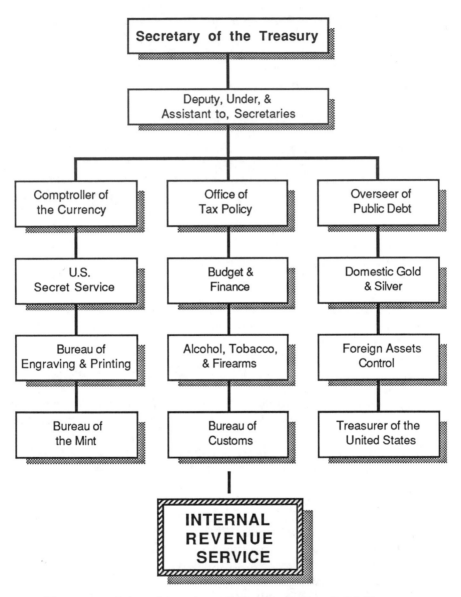

Fig. 1.1 - Other Agencies of the Department Of Treasury

Determining "Correct Tax"

Ostensibly, the sole purpose of an IRS audit is to establish (determine) the correct tax. This objective follows from the very first phrase in Section 7602(a), namely—

For the purpose of ascertaining the correctness of . . .

So, regardless of any other purpose of an audit, the statutory power of the IRS must root in the concept of ascertaining the correct tax. Establishing the correct tax is the first — and most vital — step before any other avenues of "tax administration" become applicable. If the correct tax cannot be established, the IRS is stymied. If the correct tax is less than what the IRS asserts it to be, the IRS has violated the law (which it often does).

This raises the question: What is meant by correct tax . . . and who determines it?

Despite its public image to the contrary, the IRS does not have the final say as to what constitutes the correct tax. The taxpayer (auditee) has as much say in the matter as does the IRS. Unfortunately, most auditees are not aware of this. They assume a docile, defeatist attitude that the IRS has the irrevocable and unchallengeable final say.

Whether there is a final say or not is questionable. Not every correct tax issue has a final say. If there is one, it rests in the judicial branch of government: not in the executive branch of which the IRS is part. For most bona fide tax issues, the final say rests with the U.S. Tax Court. This an entirely different agency of government, fully independent of the IRS. If an issue cannot be settled in tax court, there is the U.S. Appeals Court, and, if necesssary, the U.S. Congress itself.

Meanwhile, short of tax court proceedings, the correct tax is constructed to mean the tax which results from using all applicable tax rules and tax rates, after taking into account all facts and circumstances having a bearing on the issue. Thus, the correct tax is that which follows from a reasonable examination involving judgments of accuracy, propriety, and sufficiency. These judgments may entail comparisons, verifications, appraisals, and other pertinent facts necessary for correct deteminations.

In most audit cases, the correct tax is not a simple black or white accounting issue. There are many more grey areas than there are black and white ones. Black, white, or grey: there is often a whole chain of facts and events that must be sifted and analyzed in order to arrive at the correct bottom line (tax).

Consider, for example, a taxpayer who sells a truck (boat or airplane) used in his trade or business. What is the "correct tax" on the transaction?

The answer requires tracing a whole sequence of events. How much did he initially pay for the truck, including sales tax? Can he verify the amount claimed with a purchase invoice? What kind of depreciation writeoff did he take? Did he use an allowable method and useful life? Did he apply the allowable depreciation properly each year, in proportion to his actual business use? What was his cumulative total depreciation taken to date of sale? What were his gross sales price and selling expenses? What was his actual gain on sale, if any? If a gain, what portion is depreciation recapture and what portion is capital gain? What are his other sources of income, and what is his adjusted gross income? What is his taxable income; what is his tax rate? Of the total tax computed, what portion is represented by the sale of the truck? Is this the correct tax? If not, why not?

In the audit process, a taxpayer/auditee has as much right to present his version of the correct tax as does the IRS. A persistent auditee can keep the IRS at bay as long as necessary to arrive at reasonable correctness. So long as an auditee is progressing in good faith, he cannot be criticized, hounded, or penalized. The correct tax must be determined before the IRS can take any follow-on administrative actions.

Meaning of "Any Return"

Actually, the first phrase in Section 7602 says nothing about correct tax. It says . . . "correctness of any return." A "return" is a tax return; therefore, correct tax and correctness of any return are mutually intertwined.

The term "any return," however, is much broader in application and power by government than "correct tax." In this arena, the taxpayer/auditee is less of an equal with government. He is exposed to much greater risks of integrity, aggressiveness, and vindictiveness by government agents and examiners. Here's why.

The term "any return" means a federal tax form or schedule of *any type* subject to the laws and provisions of the Internal Revenue Code. There are some 600 official forms and schedules! Very few taxpayers are familar with all of the provisions for filing these "returns." The government could easily assert that some return was due, and the taxpayer would know nothing about it.

By far the most common return is an income tax return. But there are also gift tax returns, employer tax returns, excise tax returns, estate tax returns, fiduciary tax returns, partnership returns, corporate returns, and various information returns pertinent to federal taxation. Many of these returns are required to be filed even though there may be no tax liability. If not filed, an administrative penalty applies. Thus, there is great danger for abuse of power by the IRS in the "any return" concept.

The general rule prescribing "any return" is embodied in Section 6011: *General Requirement of Return, Statement, or List.* Subsection (a) thereof reads in full as follows:

When required by regulations prescribed by the Secretary any person made liable for any tax imposed by this title [Title 26: Internal Revenue Code], *or with respect to the collection thereof, shall make a return or statement according to the forms and regulations prescribed by the Secretary. Every person required to make a return or statement shall include therein the information required by such forms or regulations.*

In other words, the term "any return" encompasses *any person . . . liable for any tax . . .* imposed by the approximately 1,800 sections of the Internal Revenue Code. This is a big order. Not every taxpayer is aware of its all-sweeping effect. Section 6011(a) enables our "separate govenment" to set its audit traps for whomever it wants. At times, the IRS can be blatantly vindictive.

If a return is not filed when required, the Secretary — meaning the IRS — is empowered to "make a reurn" . . . for the taxpayer. This is authorized by the second phrase of Section 7602, namely:

For the purpose of . . . making a return where none has been made, . . . the [IRS] *is authorized—*

A return made by the IRS is presumed to contain the correct tax. This is a *presumption* only. Rarely is it the correct tax. It will be the maximum tax! It is based on gross income only, without any itemized deductions. Then, maximum penalties and maximum interest are added. An IRS-prepared return is punishment for not filing your own tax return when required.

In a recent case, the taxpayer had enough withholdings to come within $228 of the correct tax. Just before the April deadline for filing, the taxpayer was injured and was hospitalized off and on for several years. She did not file. Subsequently, the IRS made a return for her claiming that she owed $7,555. After a long series of complaints with supporting documents, the IRS eventually accepted the $228 as correct.

Basic Revenue Enforcement

The IRS is not in the business of helping taxpayer/auditees reduce or minimize their taxes. Nor is the IRS in the business of instructing auditees how to prepare their returns to avoid or minimze future audits. The IRS is in the tax audit business for one reason only: to rake in more revenue into the federal coffer.

Once additional revenue is raked in, the IRS has no say on how the money is disbursed. You can be sure, however, that the more it rakes in, the more favorably the IRS is viewed by members of Congress. This means that more money can be spent on govenment programs, which may not be taxpayer/voter approved. The whole financing scheme of government is ultimately contingent upon the power of audit.

Thus, the power to audit tax returns is a basic enforcement tool of the entire U.S. Treasury Department. The power to enforce an audit is embodied in the power of summons granted by Congress to the Secretary of the Treasury. We revealed this summons power previously, but we will requote it again for instructive emphasis.

The power of summons appears in Section 7602(a)(2). It reads in part:

> *The Secretary is authorized—*
> *To summon the person liable for tax or required to perform the act . . . to appear before the Secreary at a time and place named in the summons and to produce such books, papers, records, or other data, and to give such testimony, under oath, as may be relevant or material to such inquiry.*

A "summons" is an official command. It is a call by authority to appear at the place named and to attend to a duty. It is a written notification to answer and respond. A summons is not to be taken lightly. If you do not respond, it can be shoved down your throat!

The IRS uses two forms of summons: informal and formal. An informal summons is the audit notification letter mentioned in the Introduction. It is issued when a return has been filed and mechanically selected for audit. It is "informal" in the sense that a two-way cooperative endeavor is expected; it is a "routine" administrative process. We will discuss later — in much depth — the details of audit notification and your response(s) thereto.

A formal summons is a much more serious matter. It is "formal" in the sense that the language is strong and threatening. The date and time of appearance are specific, as are the information and records sought. There are dire warnings for failure to obey. The IRS means business. Any pretense of two-way cooperation is nonexistent. In such a summons, there is potential for rampant abuse of power by the IRS.

A formal summons is issued, generally, under the following circumstances:

1. Important information on a return is lacking, evasive, or grossly distorted.
2. No tax return has been filed where required.
3. Substantial sources of income from payers filing information returns have gone unreported by recipients.
4. Recalcitrant and rebellious auditees who have refused to submit relevant books, records, and papers.
5. Suspicions or reports of fraud or evasion.
6. Criminal investigations of noncompliant persons.
7. Canvassing for taxable persons and objects.
8. Enforcement measures for other departments of government.

The general format of a formal summons is presented in Figure 1.2. The presentation is highly editorialized and simplified. On its back side it cites the statutory punishment for failure to obey: a $1,000 fine or one year imprisonment, or both.

Subtle Intimidation

Let the reader clearly understand that the scope of this book is limited strictly to his or her response to audit notification letters. This is the *informal summons* process above. We believe that most auditees are conscientious taxpayers who will comply with the initial requests, without forcing the IRS to issue a formal summons. Indeed, reasonable cooperation with the IRS usually pays off.

Form 6638	SUMMONS	Department of the Treasury Internal Revenue Service

IN THE MATTER OF
THE TAX LIABILITY OF_____*(your name)*_____

Periods_____*(tax year(s))*_____

The Commissioner of Internal Revenue

TO_____*(your name)*_____

AT_____*(your address)*_____

YOU ARE HEREBY SUMMONED AND REQUIRED TO APPEAR BEFORE
(Internal Revenue Service Officer Named)

to give testimony relating to the tax liability of the person identified above, and to bring with you and produce for examination the following books, records, papers, and other data:

_____   _____
_____   _____
_____   _____
_____   _____
_____   _____

Place and Time for Appearance:

AT_____*(address of IRS office named above)*_____

ON_____*(date, time, month, year)*_____

_____*(Signature of Issuing Officer)*

**ISSUED UNDER AUTHORITY OF
THE INTERNAL REVENUE CODE**

_____*(Title)*

_____*(Date of Issue)*

Back Side

PROVISIONS OF THE INTERNAL REVENUE CODE

Sec.7602 - Examination of Books and Witnesses	Sec.7605 - Time and Place of Examination
Sec.7603 - Service of Summons	Sec.7609 - Special Procedures for Third-Party Summonses
Sec.7604 - Enforcement of Summons	Sec.7610 - Fees and Costs for Witnesses

Sec.7210 - Failure to Obey Summons : $1,000 or 1 year, or both

Fig. 1.2 - General Content of Formal IRS Summons

This does not mean that an auditee has to comply by hanging his head low, trembling in fear, and pleading for mercy. Cooperation means that he must respond as an equal and not cower as an unequal. One's selection for audit is based on probabilty factors: *not* on proven factors. The improbability factors are as much on your side as are the probability factors on the IRS's side.

Nevertheless, a stereotyped form letter with attachments coming from the IRS *is* a subtle form of intimidation. The IRS knows this, and you know it. If read carefully, there is evidence of a genuine attempt to make the audit notifications courteous and informative. Unfortunately, few auditees ever read these letters carefully. The result is that recipients are intimidated, whether the IRS officially intends so or not.

To "intimidate" means to make timid or fearful: to frighten. It also means to compel: to discourage ordinary reasoning.

The fact that an audit notification letter has no salutation is, of itself, a form of intimidation. There is no "Dear Taxpayer," no "Dear Auditee," no "Dear Selectee," nor any other humanized greeting. There is no functional title or other quick-identifying heading. Lacking these ordinary courtesies, the audit letter is instantly dehumanized. The reason for this is that the notification is an offical summons, informal though it may be.

Near the bottom end of the audit notification letter, there is a paragraph which reads—

The law requires you to substantiate all items affecting your tax liabilities when requested to do so. If you do not keep this appointment or do not arrange another, we will have to proceed on the basis of available return information.

This paragraph means that, if you do not respond, the examiner will disallow all of your expenses, deductions, and credits, and assess a tax based on your gross income only. This, of course, greatly exaggerates your tax. This is the examiner's "informal enforcement" of his/her summons notice.

The IRS gets a lot of revenue mileage out of its audit letters. Most recipients tell their friends and associates. The friends and associates, in turn, tell others. In this word-of-mouth process, many taxpayers become frightened and dismayed. The result is that many taxpayers deliberately overpay their taxes in the hope that they will not also receive an audit notification letter.

Training of IRS Personnel

There is a byproduct purpose of an audit which has little to do, per se, with correctness of tax or additional revenue. Certain returns are selected solely for their instructional benefit to audit-and-enforcement trainees.

All new IRS employees with legal, accounting, or business educational backgrounds have to go through on-the-job training. This training is best achieved in the audit (examination) division of various district offices. In these positions, they are able to derive meaningful practical experience with taxpayers of all kinds.

An audit by a trainee is tedious and time consuming. Whereas an experienced auditor may accomplish an examination in one or two hours, a trainee auditor may take 5, 6, or more hours to cover the same ground. This is because trainees are not sure of their positions, and they tend to be picky-picky. They have to check every little detail with their training supervisor, whether revenue significant or not. This is quite an imposition on the taxpayer, who either has to take time off from work or pay someone to represent him . . . for nearly a full day.

To assuage taxpayer irritations at lengthy, nit-picking audits by trainees, it is a policy of the IRS to limit trainee audit adjustments to one or two items. Although a trainee may pick up numerous changes in a return, his supervisor usually waives all but one or two. This is IRS's way of thanking a taxpayer for the more than ordinary length of time undergoing examination.

Every audit notification letter usually ends with the invitation—

Please contact the telephone number shown in the heading of this letter if you have any questions.

Certainly, there is one question you should ask: "Is this a training audit?" You are not likely to get a direct "yes" or "no" answer. You'll be told that it is a routine audit, and so forth.

If this happens, then ask, "What is the examination group number?" All examination groups are assigned a number, such as EG 2508. (The "EG" is for Examination Group.)

The IRS person answering the phone will usually tell you the EG number without hesitation. Then ask: "Is this an office audit or a field audit?"

If an office audit, you must take your books and records to the IRS office in your area. This means subjecting yourself to commute traffic, parking problems, and elevator delays. After reporting in to the IRS receptionist, you'll be told to wait. If you see a lot of other taxpayers waiting, you'll know you are in for a training audit.

If a field audit, the IRS trainee will come to your place of business or personal residence. Forget about your constitutional rights of privacy. You cannot refuse entry to an IRS auditor. Congress gave the store away in Code Section 7606(a), to wit:

The Secretary may enter, in the daytime, any building or place where any articles or objects subject to tax are made, produced, or kept, so far as may be necessary for the purpose of examining said articles or objects.

Compliance Measurement

Another byproduct purpose of an audit is the development of statistical data on the degree of taxpayer compliance. This is called a TCMP audit: **Total Compliance Measurement Program**.

This is not a picky-picky training audit. It is an exhaustive line-by-line audit of every item on the tax return. The objective is to develop data on selected groupings of taxpayers to measure their conformity or nonconformity with the tax laws. The information is used, not so much for revenue purposes, but for tracking certain types of taxpayers with the view of strengthening administrative practices. A TCMP audit is a clear-cut case where the IRS is over-stepping its statutory authority for ascertaining the correct tax.

A TCMP audit is not only time-consuming and exasperating: all pretense of reasonableness and necessariness are thrown to the wind. Nothing is taken for granted. Nothing is taken on testimony. There is no compromise. Every item on the return must be supported by valid third-party documentation. This applies to every expense, every deduction, every allowance, and every credit claimed, A TCMP audit may take anywhere from 10 to 20 hours — or more — for completion.

There have been more appeals and litigation over TCMP audits than any other process. Some lower courts have held that a taxpayer need not cooperate in a TCMP audit. Its purpose is not to determine the correct tax. Its purpose is research, not revenue.

Not surprisingly, some taxpayers have objected to being chosen for TCMP examination. In one exemplary case, *U.S. vs. Flagg*, 11/8/79 *DC-Iowa*, the lower court refused to enforce a formal summons against the taxpayer for production of his records.

Ignoring the court's order, the IRS levied a $45,000 deficiency against the taxpayer and began seizure proceedings. The IRS subsequently browbeat the higher court (the 8th Circuit Court of Appeals) to reverse the lower court and remand that it enforce the $45,000 levy [*634 F 2nd 1087: 1980*].

One of the disgraces of this country is that federal judges themselves can be intimidated by the IRS. If a federal judge is unimpressed by the IRS tactics, Justice Department attorneys (who represent the IRS in court) can become goonish. They can invoke Section 7212 and accuse the judge of interfering with the administration of tax laws.

The gist of Section 7212(a) is as follows:

Whoever . . . by force or threats of force (including any threatening letter or communication) . . . obstructs or impedes, or endeavors to obstruct or impede, the due administration of this title, shall, upon conviction thereof, be fined not more than $5,000, or imprisoned not more than 3 years, or both.

So, in a knock-down, drag-out power play between the IRS and the judiciary, the judiciary is no match. A court order adverse to IRS interests can be construed as force or threat of force interfering with the administration of tax laws.

As an overall consequence, even though a TCMP audit is clearly beyond the authority of Section 7602, the IRS gets away with it. This is because of the timidity of Congress in granting too much power to the IRS, and in not policing that power.

Penalty Pyramiding

There is one truly sinister purpose of an audit which is seldom publicized. This purpose is the generation of large amounts of additional revenue through "penalty pyramiding." This is the process of adding one tax penalty on top of another, each penalty being of increasing magnitude over the previous one. An audit provides the ideal opportunity for doing this because multiple issues, years, forms, schedules, and rules are involved. All tax penalties are sanctified as *additions to tax*. They produce a major sources of additional revenue . . . without increasing taxes. For Congress, this is political magic.

Although there have always been a few longstanding penalties for clear-cut failures to file and/or failures to pay, the growth of penalty mania accelerated in the years after 1981. There are now some 55 different tax penalties as of last count, and rising! They are incorporated in Sections 6651 through 6724 of the tax code. This batch of penalty sections is designated as: Chapter 68 — Addition to the Tax, Additional Amounts, and Assessable Penalties.

The basic authorization for penalty pyramiding is set forth in Section 6665(a)(1): *Additions Treated as Tax—*

The additions to the tax, additional amounts, and penalties provided by this chapter shall be paid upon notice and demand and shall be assessed, collected, and paid in the same manner as taxes.

This section gives a glaring green light to the IRS.

Individually, a penalty can range from a low of 5% to a high of 75%, depending on the degree of negligence, understatement, overstatement, omission, failure, or fraud asserted by the IRS. When pyramided and compounded, the penalties can double and triple the amount of underlying tax. This is too much power to grant to the personal whims of IRS officers, agents, and employees.

If we are ever to have a truly fair tax system in the U.S., Congress has got to do two things, namely:

One. For every penalty asserted, there must be an objective good-faith standard with which the IRS must comply. Such standards do not exist today.

Two. In a true democracy, there must be provisions for "reverse penalties" *against* the IRS, its officers, agents, and employees. The 2,500,000-word federal tax code is totally void on this point.

In the meantime, you as an auditee — or potential auditee — have to prepare for all sorts of unforeseens and unknowns. Our objective is to help you in this regard.

Evidence of Evasion

There is one final, important administrative purpose of a "routine" audit. It is the collection and documentation of investigatory information on tax evasion by payees. A "payee" is a person to whom an auditee pays money; the amount paid is claimed as a deduction on the return being audited. Typical payees are attorneys, contractors, doctors, salesmen, suppliers, dealers, and other persons in a trade, business, or profession. In most cases, payments to these persons are allowable deductions on appropriate schedules of the payer's (auditee's) tax return.

A deduction on a payer's return is reportable income on the payee's return. Thus, by auditing all payers (clients and customers) of the payee, the IRS can obtain hard, third-party evidence of gross income of the payee under surveillance.

Insofar as the payers are concerned, the auditing procedures are not strictly for ascertaining the correctness of tax of each auditee. The "routine" aspects are simply a pretense. The real purpose is an administrative canvassing for the taxable persons who are not filing tax returns, or who are filing returns with substantial unreported income. Rarely is an auditee aware of this purpose.

Audit canvassing is authorized by Section 7601. The general rule thereof reads, in part, as follows:

The Secretary shall, to the extent he deems it practicable, cause officers or employees of the Treasury Department to proceed, from time to time, through each internal revenue district and inquire after and concerning all persons therein who may be liable to pay any internal revenue tax . . . .

Compare this wording with that of Section 7602, previously quoted. It is much broader in scope than simply auditing for ascertaining the correct tax. It is the basic authority for gathering information on potential tax evaders.

We all try to minimize our taxes and avoid them where we can do so legitimately. Evasion, on the other hand, is the willful concealment — knowingly — of major amounts of taxable income. Willful tax evasion is a very serious matter.

The reader must understand that the scope of this book is limited to ordinary audits (for correct taxes). Evasion of tax is not at issue and will not be discussed any further. There may be some inadvertent omissions of income and understatements of tax, but willful concealment is not involved. The underlying premise in this book is that one's return is selected for audit under the specific authority of Section 7602 only.

2

THE SELECTION PROCESS

> Every Tax Return Goes To An IRS Regional Center Where It Is Screened For Acceptance And Arithmetic Accuracy. In Some Cases, Taxpayers Are Contacted For Additional Information And/Or Taxes. (These Contacts Are Not Audits.) Screened Returns Are Summary Taped And Sent To The IRS National Computer Center. There, The Tapes Are Information Matched With Payer Inputs, Nationwide. Subsequently, The Tapes Are Mechanically Scored. High-Score Returns Become Candidates For Audit. The Final Audit Selection, However, Is Made In Each Local IRS District Office.

Approximately 115,000,000 (115 million) individual tax returns are filed each year, many electronically. On average, one to three attached schedules are required per return. Thus, approximately 250,000,000 individual tax forms (pieces of paper) are involved.

Aside from individual forms, there are approximately 35,000,000 other income forms (corporations, partnerships, fiduciaries, and amendments).

There is no way in the world that the Internal Revenue Service can select and audit each and every income tax form. To do so, it would have to increase its nationwide staff more than 30-fold over its present size (approximately 120,000 officers, agents, and employees).

Obviously, the IRS has had to devise a scheme — a highly sophisticated one at that — to select from the annual tidal waves of paper those returns which offer the highest probability of additional tax revenue. Although preliminary screening techniques are used, the basic selection is by computer, using secret input formulas.

Each "secret formula" is a statistical weighting process of mathematical probabilities. We make no pretense herein of knowing what the secret formula is. We know some of the factors that go into it, but how they are scored and weighted we do not know. We can make only experienced guesses.

At the end of the line, nearly 3,000,000 individual returns are selected for audit each year. However, the selection process actually starts on the day on which a return is officially accepted at one of the IRS's regional process centers.

Procedural Mechanics

There are ten IRS regional processing centers located throughout the United States. The city, state, and postal zip of each center is published in the instructions which accompany the blank Form 1040 and schedules. All individual tax returns are posted to the center nearest where the taxpayer resides.

At each center, the Form 1040s plus schedules are screened for acceptance. Official acceptance means that a return is reasonably complete and properly signed. When accepted, a return is stamped with the date and time of official receipt.

An "acceptable return" is one which, when directed by Form 1040 itself, is accompanied by the required backup schedules. If not attached, the return or a blank schedule is sent back to the taxpayer for completion. This delays the processing time, and may even cause an otherwise timely-filed return to be late.

An acceptable return is also one which contains one or more valid signatures. A valid signature is one which is reasonably legible, and which corresponds in name or names to that on the heading of the return.

A valid signature is also required below an unaltered perjury statement. The statement reads as follows:

Under penalties of perjury, I declare that I have examined this return and accompanying schedules and statements, and to the best of my knowledge and belief, they are true, correct and complete.

Any strike-outs or insertions to this perjury statement, and/or any cute signature symbols, are cause for a return being sent back for redo and proper signaturizing.

Some taxpayers file a protest return. A "protest return" usually contains no specific dollar information on any of the income lines on Form 1040. Instead, a notation is made concerning constitutional rights, supported with attachments quoting specific court cases and IRS transgressions. Approximately 15,000 of these protest returns are filed each year.

The IRS, of course, does not recognize a protest return. While protests are indeed constitutional, they are illegal if submitted as an original return. Legitimate protests can occur only after the IRS's version of the correct tax is determined. The correct tax cannot be determined without a proper and complete return. Hence, protest returns are invariably sent back to the filer. An accompanying form letter explains the taxpayer's filing obligations, and states that the information as submitted is unacceptable.

National Computer Center

Once a return is accepted at a regional center, there is some preliminary screening and checking of the arithmetic thereon. A summary computer tape is then prepared on each taxpayer.

The summary tapes — *not* the tax returns themselves — from all ten regional centers go to the National Computer Center at Martinsburg, West Virginia. At this main center, other information is added to each taxpayer's summary tape. This "other information" comes from five years of storage data on each taxpayer, and from approximately 1,000,000,000 (1 billion) current information forms submitted by payers and notifiers. The tapes are then final processed, cleared for refunds, and score-selected for potential audit. The key items for audit are appropriately computer flagged.

Those returns selected for potential audit are put on master tapes for each of the ten regional centers. These tapes are sent back to the centers where the selectees are arranged into those geographic areas covered by the 60 Internal Revenue district offices. The math scores of the selectees, together with their original returns, are sent to the respective district offices. The final selection for audit is done at each district office.

A schematic overview of the audit selection process is presented in Figure 2.1. The arrangement is to give you a quick insight into the procedural mechanics involved. As you can see, it is primarily a

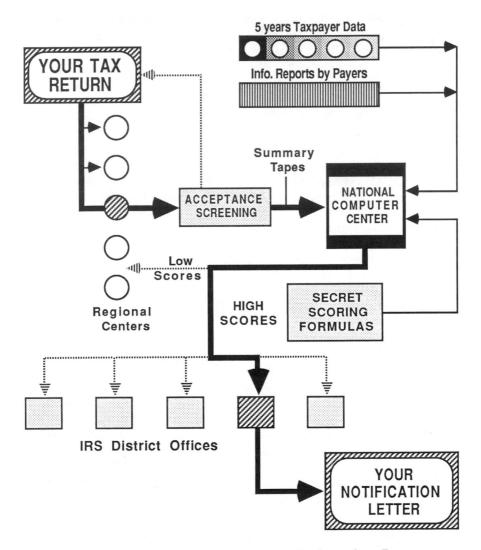

Fig. 2.1 - Schematic Overview of Audit Selection Process

mechanical selection process. There are, however, manual inputs at each process center and at each district office.

There is an appreciable lapse of time between one's return being accepted at a regional center, and being selected for audit at a district office. Typically, this lapse is from 18 to 36 months after a return is filed. The discussion which follows will make more obvious why this amount of time is necessary.

Eyeball Screening

The acceptance of a return at a regional center does not mean, necessarily, that it is sufficiently complete for immediate computer processing. Before it is released into the computer mechanics, there is a preliminary eyeball screening given to each return. That is, human beings — with human eyeballs — actually look at the returns. They do not read them; they simply scan and screen them. The eyeball screening is a four-stage process as follows:

Stage 1. Line-by-line scanning of pages 1 and 2 of Form 1040, to verify if all required schedules, statements, and forms are attached.

Stage 2. Detachment and scanning of attachments to verify if official forms, or officially approved substitute forms, are used.

Stage 3. Screening of Form 1040 and all attachments for unallowed deductions and unallowed credits.

Stage 4. Coding the return in preparation for ADP (Automatic Data Processing).

Excluding the heading and signature blocks, there are approximately 60 line spaces for numerical entries on Form 1040. Not every line space on every return will contain an entry figure. But of those entries made, an attached schedule or form may or may not be required. If a designated schedule or form is required to be attached, the screener expects to find it.

For example, there is a line on page 1 of Form 1040 which reads as:

Other gains or losses (attach Form 4797)

If there is an entry figure in this line, there had better be a Form 4797 attached. If not, the taxpayer will be contacted and requested to provide it. Meanwhile, his return is set aside until a response is received. If no response is received in 30 to 60 days, a "red flag" symbol will be entered on the return and the screening will be resumed.

Some taxpayers supply attachments and statements which are not specifically requested. For example, "Adjustments to Income" on Form 1040 includes a line which reads simply:

Recipient's SSN: _____ Alimony paid $_____
(SSN is Social Security Number)

No attachment is required. There is no need to attach an explanation of when you were divorced or why. There is no need to attach your property settlement terms. The computer cannot read unofficial statements or forms.

Where there are proper attachments, the screener scans them hurriedly for unallowable deductions. For example, if one takes 100% of all his medical expenses, it is not allowed. It has to be reduced by 7.5% of one's adjusted gross income. If one takes a casualty or theft loss without deducting insurance reimbursement plus 10% AGI (adjusted gross income), it is not allowed. If one claims business meals and entertainment, he must subtract 50%. If no subtraction, the item is not allowed.

The final phase of the eyeball screening is coding the return in preparation for its computer summary tape. For this purpose, a 14-digit "Document Locator Number" (DLN) is assigned. This is followed by other coded digits which classify the return either as a business return or a nonbusiness return. A business return is where the primary source of income is from a trade, business, or profession, including partnerships, farming, and fishing.

After classification, each line entry on a return is "brown penciled" (actually) to instruct the key punch operators what to do. In those cases where an entry is illegible or ambiguous, the screener will brown pencil that figure which produces the highest tax. The return is then released to the key punch department (ADP) where the summary tape is made.

Arithmetical Corrections

The first step in ADP (Automatic Data Processing) is computer scanning of each Form 1040 for indexing information. The foremost index, of course, is one's social security number. This is followed by filing status (single, joint, married separate, head of household, qualifying widow(er)), and by number of exemptions. The information helps to assure the correct tax computation.

Also computer scanned are the little checkboxes on the return. There are approximately 25 of these checkboxes on Form 1040. Most taxpayers do not even realize they are there. They alert the computer to certain line entries and cross-checking subroutines for summary computations.

After the index scanning, the 1040 and attachments are turned over to key-punch operators. These operators are prohibited from reading or interpreting any information on a return. They are human robots. They are controlled by a horizontal guider which feeds down each page of return, line by line. Wherever there is a line entry, the operator punches in that numerical figure. Each line entry is then automatically programmed into the computer.

The operators punch in only what is called "entry information." A taxpayer's additions, subtractions, divisions, and multiplications are ignored. These are arithmetic functions which the computer will do on its own. The exception is the total tax figured by the taxpayer, and his/her computations of the amount of tax overpayment or balance due. These bottom-line items are used for comparison with the computer summary printouts.

One of the true marvels of computer technology is the rapidity of arithmetic computations . . . virtually free from error. With proper indexing and entry data, the arithmetically "correct tax" is displayed instantly. Simultaneously, any corrections to overpayment or balance due are printed out.

If the computer correct tax and the taxpayer's tax differ, a correction notice is automatically sent out. There are several forms of computer correction notices, depending on the classification of a return. The most formidable notice is headed: **Correction Notice — Balance Due IRS**. You pay the balance due or else. You have no opportunity to protest; you have no opportunity to correct the computer. You may, however, correct any error in your name, address, and social security number.

The general format of a balance due correction notice is presented in Figure 2.2. It is a highly edited version of several computer printout forms, so the arrangement is not official, though the gist is.

If you scrutinize the official computer messages, you will find wording to the effect:

Department of Treasury **Internal Revenue Service** **(Regional Center)** YOUR NAME & ADDRESS	Date of Notice _____ Social Security No. _____ Document Locator _____ Tax Form _____ Tax Year Ending _____ Call or Write To _____

CORRECTION NOTICE - BALANCE DUE IRS
Make payable to Internal Revenue Service
Make payment within 10 days of above date

Correction Explanation

Very short sentence
printout by computer.

Rarely sufficient
explanation.

Compare with "tax due"
details on right.

· ·

Detach stub below
and return with
payment or inquiry

Tax Statement

Tax on Return _____
Corrected Tax on Return _____
Tax Withheld _____
Estimated Payments _____
Other Credits _____
Other Payments _____
Total Payments & Credits _____
Unpaid Tax .... _____
Penalty .... _____
Interest .... _____

Balance Due IRS | $ |

Payment Stub

Fig. 2.2 - General Format of Arithmetic Correction Notice

Allow for enough mailing time to be sure that we receive your payment by 10 days from date of this notice. Otherwise, additional penalties and interest will accrue.

This does not give you adequate time to check the computer computations with your copy of your tax return. The key punch robots could make an error (and often do). Your eyeball screener could misread a line entry and code it wrong (which often happens). IRS operators mispunch computer keys all the time.

Many taxpayers think that an arithmetic correction notice or request for a specific attachment constitutes an audit of their return. This is not so. These are purely preliminary screening matters. A correction notice is simply that. It is an arithmetic correction only. It has nothing whatsoever to do with preselection for audit.

Information Matching

As depicted in Figure 2.1, the summary tapes prepared at a regional center go to Martinsburg, West Virginia. It is at Martinsburg that Big Brother really gets going. Here, some 115,000,000 human taxpayers are on master tapes. For each taxpayer, there are five years of tape-stored information. These master tapes are backed up with microfilm records on each taxpayer, where applicable, going back nearly 20 years.

Into the Martinsburg center, various "information forms" are fed. These are not tax returns; they are income information reports submitted (under threat of penalties) by payers and notifiers. There are approximately 1,000,000,000 (1 billion) of these information forms submitted each year. Most of these income reports have each taxpayer's social security number on them. Where a social security number is missing, the taxpayer's name and address are used.

The information reports are made on three official series of forms, namely:

> **Series W-2.** Statements of wages, salaries, pensions, bonuses, gambling winnings, annuity payments, and other income (such as social security benefits received).
> **Series 1099.** Statements for recipients of broker transactions, liquidating distributions, original issue discounts, interest, dividends, medical and health care payments, unemployment compensation, state tax refunds, nonemployee compensation, and miscellaneous income from rents, royalties, prizes, and awards.
> **Series K-1.** Distributive share of income from partnerships, estates, trusts, and small business corporations.

The very first computer activity at Martinsburg is a matching of the information reports with the income actually reported on each Form 1040. This is called IMP: **Information Matching**

Program (coded as CP-2000). This is a highly sophisticated procedure which only advanced multibillion-dollar computers can do. The system is so refined now that well over 90% of all individual summary tapes are information matched. The few that escape matching do so only because of foulups in tax identifying numbers (TIN's).

The IRS's CP-2000 program is so refined now that a 10 cent — yes 10 *cent* — mismatch can generate $66.96 in penalties and interest. Yes, we have a photocopy of the official documentation thereon. It's DLN number is 99212-105-54149-5 (14 digits).

Be fully aware, however, that the CP-2000 printouts have an error rate of nearly 35%. Yes, this is so. These IRS errors arise because of bureaucratic inertia and greed: the perfect ingredients for sloppy administration. The IRS will *not read* a taxpayer's return to find out for itself where its own errors are. Nor is there any in-house policing to verify the accuracy of the printouts before they are sent to an intimidated public. The IRS wants your money above everything else in this world.

Audit Based on DIF Scores

There are approximately 20,000,000 computer notices of deficiency that go out each year. A CP-2000 deficiency is still not an audit, though most taxpayers think it is. Functionally, it is a preliminary screening at Martinsburg before the real audit selection process begins.

Actual audit selection is based on a DIF-scoring process. The "DIF" means: **Discriminate Information Function**. A discriminate function is computer jargon for probability theory. One's DIF score is a measure of statistical probability that additional revenue can be garnisheed into federal coffers.

DIF-scoring involves various secret formulas of summary tape evaluation, weighting probabilities, and special inputs. Many fair-haired and high-IQ mathematicians are assigned to DIF formulation activities. DIF formulators are often hypnotized with their own self-brilliance and infallibility.

After the IMP matching above, all summary tapes are sent through the DIF-scoring computer. This is a cold-blooded statistical measuring process, beyond human manipulation. In the DIF procedures, there is no way in the world that a taxpayer-to-be-harassed can be singled out and preassigned some audit-range DIF score. The scoring process is truly a mechanical one, pure and simple. All the paranoia that certain taxpayers are being picked on (at Martinsburg) is without foundation.

The exact DIF-scoring range is not publicly known. To illustrate the mechanical processing involved, let us assume that the range is from 1 to 699. (Be fully aware that 1-699 is an *assumption* only.) Scores of 1 to 99 are virtually audit proof, whereas scores of 600-699 are virtually guaranteed audit.

The DIF score for each tax return is printed out on separate internal forms. The taxpayer never sees these forms. They are indexed to social security numbers, document locator numbers, secret formulas, source codes, cycle codes, and output scores.

In an overall sense, DIF-scoring is no more than a mechanical means of prioritizing those returns with the greatest potential for audit examinations.

DIF Input Considerations

Whenever there is government secretiveness, human nature bristles with suspicion. Taxpayers have to disclose everything; why can't the government do likewise? What are *they* trying to hide?

There is good reason for secretiveness of the DIF-scoring formulas. If they were made public, computer sharpies in private industry would push guaranteed audit-proof tax services. Preparer fees would then become unconscionable. Audit avoidance would become a major underground industry, similar to drug smuggling, organized crime, and gambling syndication.

Nevertheless, conscientious taxpayers are entitled to some description of the makeup and considerations that go into the DIF formulas. There are several of these formulas, estimated at about 15 in number. They are geared to various taxpayer profiles. A "profile" is an occupational grouping with more than ordinary likelihood of engaging in substantial tax avoidance efforts.

For example, criminal attorneys expert in underworld power schemes are prime profile suspects. These often are persons of exceptional ego and gall. They will take on the government at any level, for any reason, just for the excitement of entangling the system. Trial tactics in tax courts or in federal courts do not phase them one bit. They are adversary masters skillful in hiding their income in domestic trust funds and/or foreign bank accounts. The IRS has to be especially careful in its DIF formulations of these persons and their occupational associates.

Other profile suspects are subcontractors, coin-operated and cash-deal businesses, highly-paid professionals (doctors, entertainers), persons with access to great quantities of money (cashiers, bankers, brokers), dealers in credit and commercial paper, persons skilled in computer programming, tax preparers, and others. Each occupational grouping is broken down into income levels, operating experience, geographical influences, lifestyles, and personal characteristics.

For each profile, there is a "normalizing band" of personal deductions, exemptions, and credits. That is, with some 20 years of audit statistics at its computer tips, the DIF formulators have prepared accurate percentages of deductible items on a return which are ordinary and acceptable for specific income groupings. Deductions which exceed these percentages are "out of norm." The extent of out-of-normalcy is graduated into higher and higher DIF scoring points.

Multiple sources of income constitute another DIF scoring consideration. A return with one or two sources of income only is less a candidate for audit than a return with eight to ten sources of income. Multiple sources of income imply complex affairs with many temptations for overclaiming expenses. Expenses offset income and thereby reduce the tax thereon.

Expense ratios of various sources have been averaged over the years. An "expense ratio" is the total business expense of an activity divided by its gross income. All income sources have certain acceptable ratios. If these ratios are exceeded, graduated DIF points are scored.

Prime tax issues are separately DIF weighted. A "prime issue" is one towards which the IRS becomes bull-headed and/or paranoid. So-called abusive tax shelters are one example. The IRS is truly paranoid on travel expenses, business entertainment, and business use of personal autos. Other prime issues include casualty and theft losses, bad debts, attorney fees, business insurance, negative cash flow activities, stock options, sale of precious metals, and transactions over $100,000.

And to all of the statistical inputs above, the DIF formulators apply a "coefficient of variation." They apply this coefficient to each income grouping and to each income source. A coefficient of variation is the standard error of a DIF band expressed as a percentage of the DIF band. It is used to establish the *confidence factor* that the IRS has in its Martinsburg DIF scoring system.

In an IRS publication on statistics of individual income tax returns — Pub. 79 (3-81) — the IRS reveals that it has attained a DIF confidence factor of 68%. That is, it expects at least 68% of all returns audited to produce additional revenue. Ultimately, it hopes to achieve a DIF confidence of 90%. Pure mechanical selection alone will never be able to guarantee additional revenue for every return audited.

Final Selection at District Offices

As you should sense from the above, DIF scoring is not an exact science. The IRS itself does not have 100% confidence in it. As a result, final selection of a return for audit is not done at the Martinsburg Computing Center. Such selection is done at 60 district offices by experienced humans making judgmental reviews.

If the DIF-scoring range is 1-699 as *assumed* previously, it follows that scores of 300 and above would be classed as high-DIF returns. Correspondingly, those 299 and less would be low-DIF returns.

Score sheets on the high-DIF returns are sent to the regional centers from which the summary tapes came. The regional centers, in turn, send the score sheets *and* the actual tax returns to their respective district offices.

At each district office, there is an RPM staff: **Returns Program Management**. A staff member, usually quite experienced, eyeballs each high-DIF return. An audit assignment checksheet is prepared. The RPM reviewer goes down every entry on its attached schedules, statements, and forms. He attempts to satisfy himself whether a return will survive audit scrutiny.

Just because a return has a high DIF score does not mean necessarily that it will be selected for audit. If such a return has all the relevant entries, all the required attachments, with off-line annotations which are self-explanatory, convincingly prepared, there is a good chance that it will not be assigned to audit. The RPM staffers are highly manhour conscious.

Every district office has an audit production quota. The quota is in dollars of additional revenue per audit manhour. Such quotas — also called "performance standards" — are not publicized. The existence of quotas is vehemently denied by the IRS. Yet, it is our belief that these quotas run between $300 and $500 per audit hour.

In other words, an RPM staffer judges the scope of a high-DIF return in nominal audit hours. Then he judges the potential additional revenue that might be produced. If he feels that his auditors can match or exceed the quota dollars, the return is assigned for audit. If he judges below quota, the return is sent back to the regional center for data storage.

Just because a return has a low DIF score does not mean that it will escape audit altogether. Low DIF returns are subject to *special audit selection.* Candidates for special selection originate from the regional center during the preliminary screening process. Screened returns that are questionable are "red flagged" (symbolically speaking). If the return gets a high DIF score from Martinsburg, the red flagging is meaningless. If a low DIF score, red flagging becomes important; it signifies the need for special attention.

Your Chances of Audit?

Apart from the procedural aspects above, most taxpayers are concerned only with their own chances of audit. Ideally we all would like guarantees against an audit. Audits consume valuable time. But guarantees are not possible.

The best that one can expect is some estimate of the reasonable probability of an audit. To a large extent, much of such probability depends on one's adjusted gross income (AGI), multiple sources of income, and on his occupational profile.

For AGIs less than $35,000 there is a less than 1% chance of audit. For AGIs over $150,000 there is an approximate 3% chance of audit. For AGIs over $85,000 with multiple sources of income, prime issues, and targeted profiles, there is a 3-5% chance of audit. Active, entrepreneurial taxpayers are "just naturally" more prone to audits than are low-profile taxpayers.

The reason that high-profile, high-income returns are more prone to audit is simply a calculated revenue matter. Persons with AGIs less than $35,000 contribute only 18% to the total tax revenue of the federal government. Persons with AGIs more than $85,000 contribute 28% to the total revenue. Thus, it is more profitable to focus audit attention on higher-income taxpayers.

The IRS is not the least bit interested in conducting audits to educate taxpayers, nor to assist them in reducing their taxes. Other than training, research, and investigatory activities, audits are expected to produce additional revenue. Consequently, final audit selection is based on the amount of anticipated revenue per audit-hour bang.

As an overall national average, approximately 3% of all individual tax returns are audited each year (about 5% for businesses). Though low in percentage, the additional revenue produced is well in excess of $7,000,000,000 (7 *billion*)! Add another 2 to 3 billion for penalties and interest. This is a good batting average for the District audit selection process.

There is one difficulty with the probability percentages above. Using the percentages cited, no one particular taxpayer ever knows for sure whether he is in or out of the audit selection band. This is the way it is — and always will be — with statistical probabilities.

Selection by Vendetta

Lest we have given you the impression that 100% of all auditees are selected strictly on the basis of statistical probabilities, we should touch on the seamy side of the selection process. Nearly 2% of the auditees are selected for IRS vendetta reasons. Certain IRS officers, agents, and employees are addicted to power and want to prove who is boss. Yes, we know, the IRS will deny this, but it is true.

Vendetta selectees are usually professional-level taxpayers who have the intellect and stamina to stand up to IRS bullying and challenge its interpretation of a tax law. These challengers are attorneys, doctors, accountants, tax preparers, actuaries, appraisers, engineers, and teachers. Also included are persons of public prominence, and those who have complained to Congress or to the President concerning IRS misbehavior. If any of these challengers get under the skin of the power addicts in the IRS, they will be "specially selected" for audit (at the District level). For these selectees, their DIF scores are irrelevant. The IRS goes after them like a pit bull . . . with thirst for kill.

Vendetta selectees have no chance whatsoever of winning their audit on an objective, good-faith interpretation of the applicable tax law. Almost invariably, they are charged with tax fraud, and pyramided penalties are heaped onto them "to teach them a lesson." Invariably, also, these audits wind up in U.S. Tax Court . . . which can drag on and on. It can take from 5 to 10 years — yes, *years* — before a vendetta auditee is out of the woods.

From these vendetta audits, however, new IRS law emerges. This is called the *Power Addiction Law*. The essence of this law is—

*You, Mr. Taxpayer, are wrong. Do it my way . . . or else I'll
assert fraud and all other penalties against you I can think of.*

Should an IRS agent start threatening you — sometimes,
actually, by *shouting* at you — with the 75% civil fraud penalty,
you know you have a power addict on your hands. Any assertion
of fraud opens up **6 years** of your returns for audit, and allows the
IRS to go back for as many as 10 years looking for "patterns" of
fraud.

Assertions of fraud can be made by an IRS agent, based strictly
on his/her personal whim and vindictiveness. You don't believe
this? Ask your own tax professional to cite to you any regulations
or objective standards that the IRS has to follow, when alleging
fraud under Section 6663: *Imposition of Fraud Penalty*. He'll
find no regulations or objective standards whatsoever! Test us; go
check it out.

Allegations of fraud without any official guidelines promulgated
by the IRS is the dirty side of tax enforcement through the audit
process. This leads to abuse of power which the IRS is totally inept
at correcting on its own.

The whole point that we are tying to make here is that not all
audit selections are based on calculated additional revenue
probabilities. In a few instances, pure vindictiveness and pure
punitive motives prevail. These instances, in IRS parlance, are just
occasional "administrative aberrations" in the complex world of
federal taxation.

Audit Notification Letters

No matter how or on what grounds a taxpayer is selected for
audit, he/she/they will receive a written notification letter. It will not
be conspicuously identified as such, but it will be something in
writing. In some cases, you may get a post card or phone call ahead
of time, followed by a written confirmation.

Audit notification letters seem to come in all forms with no
particular styling. Much depends on the IRS practice in the locally
assigned IRS office. About the only commonality is that at the top
of the written page will appear—

*Department of the Treasury
Internal Revenue Service
District Director*

The opening sentence will read in one of several ways, namely:

1. *Your Federal income tax return has been selected for examination.*

2. *Your Federal tax return for the above year has been assigned to me for examination.*

3. *We selected your Federal income tax return for the year(s) shown below to examine the items checked at the end of this letter.*

The letter has no kind of quick-identification heading. Much criticism has been leveled at the IRS for this negligence. There is

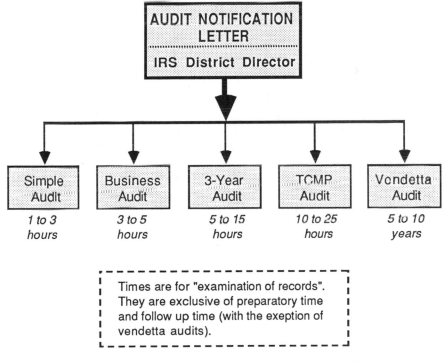

Fig. 2.3 - **Types of Audits and Examination Times**

only one reason for failing to show such a heading as Audit Notification, Notice of Selection for Audit, or Notice of Appearance for Examination. It is more intimidating to keep a taxpayer guessing as to what the District Director's letter is all about.

In the past, these letters were seldom ever signed. But in response to angry complaints against this lack of ordinary business courtesy, District Directors now permit their facsimile signatures to be used. Still, many of the facsimiles are so illegible that you cannot identify the District Director by name.

Nevertheless, over 3,000,000 (3 million) audit notification letters go out to individual taxpayers each year. The end result is that each person so notified will be subjected to one of several different types of audits, as depicted in Figure 2.3. Note in figure 2.3 that we also show the approximate audit times involved. At the minimum, three *items* in a selected year will be examined. At the maximum, all items on three *years* of returns will be examined. This is why there is no such thing as a "routine audit."

Upon receipt of a letter, you are expected to telephone within 10 days to set a date for your audit. You may set the appointment as much as 30 days from the date of your phone call, or further out, if the auditor agrees. Do not ignore making the telephone call. If you do not phone, all your deductions will be disallowed and maximum penalties will be assessed.

The letter will inform you that you may have an attorney, a certified public accountant, an individual enrolled to practice before the Internal Revenue Service, or a qualified unenrolled individual to represent you, or accompany you. So, if you are terrified or do not want to make the phone call yourself, have a *tax representative* do it for you. Professional representatives do this all the time.

3

POSITIVE ATTITUDE

Many Taxpayers Assume A Defeatist Attitude When They Receive An Audit Notification Letter. This Is Wrong And Politically Dangerous For Our Country. Winning An Audit Starts With A Positive Attitude. This Necessitates Phoning For An Appointment In A Timely Manner, And Rereading The Notification For Checked-Box Issues. Taxpayers Have Certain Rights During Audit, One Of Which Is To Be Treated Courteously And Reasonably. Good Preparation Truly Works Magic.

The average 3% probability of audit mentioned in the previous chapter is a *per year* event. As our tax-life years roll by, this probability mounts and mounts. Over a lifetime of filing income tax returns, every taxpayer — sooner or later — will face the prospect of an audit.

Most income producers commence filing tax returns at about age 20. They continue to file up into retirement and beyond . . . to about age 85. In this 65-year span of tax filings, it is almost a certainty that those over $35,000 will receive at least one audit notification letter. Some taxpayers may receive as many as ten such notifications in a lifetime.

As government becomes more computer sophisticated, we can expect a lot more tax "communications" from the Internal Revenue Service. As we tried to explain previously, not every computer printout is notification of an audit. Much of it is routine screening for acceptability of returns, corrections of arithmetic, and matching of income information. These are not — repeat, *not* — audit proceedings. Unfortunately, many taxpayers are so terrified of our "separate government" — the IRS — that they construe every computer form sent to them as being an audit.

Regardless of form, each audit notification letter is quite specific in its opening sentence. In one variant or another, the letter will state—

*Your Federal tax return . . . selected for **examination**.*

The word "examination" means "audit."

So, unless the IRS communication uses the word "examination," you are not under audit. Any other communication that you may have received is no pre-indication of an audit.

Get Your Act Together

Upon receipt of audit notification, many taxpayers literally go to pieces. When opening the envelope, their first reaction is puzzlement and confusion. Since there is no quick-identifying heading, recipients simply cannot figure out what it is all about, especially if they have never seen an audit notification before.

After frenzied scanning of the notification, they begin to sense something big. Their eyes jump around, latching onto such phrases as "examining your Federal return," "about the records needed," "the law requires taxpayers to," "about your appeal rights," "about repetitive examinations," "about your appointment," "within 10 days," . . . and so on.

At this point, utter panic ensues. Each phrase triggers a whole barrage of things to do "within 10 days." Minds spin and whirl and go out of control. In many cases, mental blocks and blanks occur. There are cold sweat and nervous twitches. It is simply too over-whelming to try to do so many things in such a short time.

If this experience happens to you, our first advice is — DO NOT PANIC! Get your act together. Remember, *you* are paying *their* salaries; "they" are not contributing one penny to your income. So, get with it. Big Brother is not your god.

It is truly shameful the way some taxpayers behave when they discover that they are under audit. They mumble in fear and fright. They immediately assume a defeatist attitude. They will pay anything to government, just to "get it over with."

Defeatism is the very ingredient that makes Big Government and Little People. This is the pathway to socialism, communism, dictatorships, and all the other "ism" governments where people are enslaved and overtaxed.

Selection for audit is not the end of your world. On the contrary, it is your opportunity to begin developing backbone and spunk. You will be a better citizen, taxpayer, and voter after an audit than before one. You will learn some things about government that you never read or hear in the news media nor in the political arena. It'll be a "one-on-one" experience for you.

Selection for audit is an opportunity to prevail; it is not a moment of defeat. It is a moment at which you can begin discovering yourself, and develop the kind of character and self-esteem to which you aspire.

Now, slow down that whizzing mind of yours. Take a few deep breaths. Look up into the sky . . . out into the universe. The Creator did not make the Earth in its present form in ten days. It took time, lots of time: thousands and millions of years. You, too, can take time to get into positive gear.

The within-10-day bit in the audit notification letter is the time allowed you to phone for an appointment. It is not the time within which you must complete the audit and pay additional tax, if any. It is simply the time within which you should acknowledge receiving the notification letter. So, go to bed and sleep for nine nights before you do anything.

We mean it. Note the date of the audit letter, then wait nine days and nights before you do anything. You will be surprised how much more determined to win you'll become.

Do Phone for Appointment

Actually, the IRS makes it easier than most agencies for phoning them. In the right-hand upper portion of each audit letter, the telephone number for contact is given. It is complete with area code and location. This not just a bureaucratic formality. It is a convenience for the auditee and is intended as such.

Once you have received an audit notification letter, there is no excuse for not phoning. If you dial correctly, the respondent will probably answer:

Internal Revenue Service . . . How may I help you?

Most IRS respondents are courteous on the phone. Many are appointment clerks: not auditors. They are not itching to throw their weight around.

You must, of course, identify yourself and give the date of the letter that you received. Allow the respondent a few moments to find the "file copy" of your notification letter. You are not the only one who has been so notified. The respondent has a file of hundreds of other taxpayers similarly selected for audit.

Your purpose in phoning is two-fold. One, to acknowledge receipt of the audit letter. Two, to set at least a tentative appointment date and time. That's all. The purpose is not to question why you are being audited; you can question later. Nor are you to start giving the IRS respondent a piece of your mind. The respondent's duty is to set an appointment date and time: no more, no less.

Chances are, even if you were immediately ready for audit — this being your 3rd or 5th audit — and wanted an appointment the next day, you could not get one. Each auditor has a case load calendar of his/her own. Auditors are usually booked three to four weeks ahead. Consequently, suggest an appointment date about 30 days from the date of your phone call.

The respondent will then check the audit calendar for that date, or for a day or two either side. Next the respondent will ask: "What hour would you like?"

Give some specific preference, like early morning, late morning, early afternoon, or late afternoon. It does not hurt to explain your business. You may have to take time off from work or leave your place of business. You may want to avoid commute traffic or take advantage of your lunch break. Quite often, the appointment clerk will try to work you into that time most convenient for you.

Aways agree to at least a tentative date, even though you may have no intention of keeping it. You can call again a week before your appointment and have it postponed. You should have some plausible reason for the postponement, however. The IRS's policy is to allow two postponements for reasonable cause, without hassle. After the second postponement, you are expected to show up.

After 30 Days: In Default

Surprisingly, perhaps, the IRS is quite tolerant when setting up the first appointment date following the mail-out of its audit notification letters. The letters state "within 10 days" but, actually, you have longer than that. The IRS takes no administrative follow-up until after 30 days from the date of notification.

The 30 days are in part due to administrative inertia, and in part due to events in a practical world.

Even though the notification letter may be stamped with a specific date, it may sit in a clerk's "out basket" 10 days or more before it gets into the mail system. Then, of course, there may be delays and disruptions in the mail service. Upon delivery, the audit selectee may be out of town temporarily, away on vacation, or he may have moved to a new address. All of these possibilities are taken into account in the 30-day grace period.

The 10 days mentioned in the notification letter are a "stimulator." One is not liable to forget something if he is instructed to do it within 10 days. If given 30 days in writing, in all probability one would set the notification letter aside. Then it could escape his memory altogether.

If 30 days have elapsed and you have not phoned for an audit appointment, you are in default. The usual procedure thereafter is to send you a Report of Examination Change, with the request that you sign the space below "Balance Due."

This constitutes what is called a *default audit*. You have defaulted in your appointment opportunity and therefore additional tax is due. The amount sought is designed to shock you.

In the original notification letter, you were told that—

If you do not keep this appointment or do not arrange another, we will have to proceed on the basis of available information on your return.

How does the IRS determine the amount of balance due? Very simply. It has the power to say "No."

It disallows all deductions, all exemptions, all credits, and all expenses that you claimed on your return. This is what is meant by "basis of available information." If you are employed, the only information available is your W-2 income statements. Any deductions that you may have claimed are not available since you did not report for audit to substantiate them. Your tax is recomputed accordingly.

For example, suppose your total sources of W-2 and interest income were $35,000 and your legitimate deductions were $15,000. The taxable income you figured on your return would be $20,000

($35,000 less $15,000). The taxable income shown on the default audit would be $35,000 (zero deductions).

If you do not respond to the Report of Examination Change within another 30 days, the tax increase is assessed. Thereupon, your case is turned over to Collections. It is no longer an examination (audit) matter. When turned over to Collections, the auditor chalks up a big revenue bonus against his hourly quota standard.

If you are in business for yourself where no W-2 has been issued, and the initial audit notification requested verification of your income, you may receive, in effect, a Notice to Produce Books and Records. It will be in threatening form called a Summons. We mentioned the summons power of the IRS back in Chapter 1. The IRS has to do this. After all, how can a balance due be determined if they do not know what your income is?

If you do not respond to the Summons, the auditor can estimate your income based on a single inquiry to a single payer of yours. When you see that estimate of your income, it will totally horrify you. And so will the tax assessed thereon.

The message above should be clear. At the very latest, do not let 30 days elapse between the date of your audit notification letter, and the date you phone in for an appointment. If you do, you have only yourself to blame for the consequences. Even governments have the right to limit their patience with procrastinators and delinquents.

Reread and Gear Up

After you make your audit appointment go back and read carefully the notification letter. Read it slowly and deliberately. Glean the *sense* of each paragraph as you go along. Read the front side and the back side in full.

Having done so, go back and reread the notification letter again. This time, concentrate on that paragraph which starts with—

About the records needed to examine your return . . .

And be sure to reread the support paragraph that starts with—

We examine returns to verify the correctness of income, exemptions, credits, and deductions . . .

For simple audits, there will be an attachment with about 50 little checkboxes. Some of the checkboxes will have preprinted subjects alongside of them, such as Contributions, Interest, Medical Expenses, and so on. Some of the boxes will have blank spaces alongside so that the auditor can type in or handwrite in those items which he (or she) wants to examine.

Note only the checkboxes with an X-mark or a √-mark. These are the specific items that the auditor wants to see. Do not waste your time or spin your wheels on the other checkboxes. Dig in and gear up for the marked ones only.

For business audit letters, there also will be an attachment. The checkboxes will be fewer in number than for simple audits, but they will be more awe-inspiring. A menu listing of the checkboxes for business audit letters, as edited, is presented in Figure 3.1. You should read the listing. It will give you an idea of the scope and depth that some audits can entail.

Most auditors are reasonable and decent. They signify this by showing more blank checkboxes than those marked with their X or √-mark. In fact, a way to pregauge your auditor is to count the number of marked boxes and compare with the total number of boxes applicable to your return. If the number of marked boxes is less than 50% of the applicable total, you probably have a reasonable auditor; one who is more likely to be understanding.

Unfortunately, some auditors get carried away with their power and authority in government. They will check *all the boxes* on the attachment! This is your tipoff that the auditor is either lazy, inexperienced, overzealous, or an outright tyrant. You cannot tell which.

If all the boxes are checked, your first recourse is to contact the auditor himself/herself by phone. You have every right to do this because the very last paragraph of your notification letter says: "If you have any questions . . . ." You certainly do.

Once your appointment is made, a specific auditor is assigned. Contact him and plead the problem of time: precious time. There is no way that you can produce all of those checked-box records (as in Figure 3.1) in any reasonable period of time.

As tactfully as you can — and hopefully in control of your emotions — find out what is *the* most pressing item on the auditor's mind. There may be more than one item pressing. You want to cooperate, but you want some reasonableness on the auditor's part too. However, don't expect too much.

For Year Under Examination, Have Available:

☐ Books and records to verify all income and expenses on Schedule C (Profit or Loss from Business or Profession).

☐ Books and records to verify all sales and cost basis on Schedule D (Capital Gains and Losses).

☐ Books and records to verify all income and expenses on Schedule E (Supplemental Income Schedule).

☐ Books and records to verify all income and expenses on Schedule F (Farm Income and Expenses).

☐ All personal and business checks written during the year.

☐ Monthly bank statements for the months of December____ through January____ for all personal and business accounts.

☐ Passbooks or statements for all savings accounts, savings certificates, certificates of deposits, money market funds, etc.

☐ Information to show balances at beginning and end of year for all personal and business loans and debts.

☐ Records to substantiate all accounts receivable at end of year.

☐ Records to substantiate all accounts payable at end of year.

☐ All brokerage records, including monthly brokerage statements of account, and confirmation of sales and purchases of securities.

☐ Purchase invoices on all vehicles and equipment used for business, acquired during the year.

☐ Sales contracts on all vehicles and equipment used for business, sold or exchanged during the year.

☐ Settlement statements on all real property acquired or disposed of during the year and/or prior years, as applicable.

Fig. 3.1 - Menu of Checkbox Items for Business Audits

If you get no satisfaction and the auditor insists on all of the checkboxes, then request the name of his/her supervisor. Ask to speak to that supervisor. If necessary, call back.

An IRS supervisor will not arbitrarily overrule one of his/her auditors. However, being a little more qualified, the supervisor may be more helpful in answering your questions and in appearing more reasonable as to what is expected in the audit. Again, of course, you plead precious time. You simply cannot — and will not — do everything at the snap of their finger.

Your Rights During Audit

Before going to your audit appointment, it is a good idea to touch base with the local office of your Congressman. Whether you voted for him or not, you are one of his constituents and are entitled to the services of his staff.

Congressional staff persons are very personable men and women, and are very responsive to constituent complaints about government agencies. Every Congressman has at least one staff member who is a specialist in procedure on complaints against the IRS. Get the name and phone number of that person. Write it on a *little card* and tuck it in one of your pockets before going to audit.

Your basic rights during an audit are woven into the notification letter which, by now, you should have read several times. As you have come to realize, your rights are not specifically delineated in 1, 2, 3 fashion. They are somewhat obscured. Therefore, let us list these rights without all of the administrative legalese.

One. *You have the right to be presumed honest.*
In an ordinary audit, it is presumed that you are honest and not engaged in any criminal activity. If you have claimed an item that you cannot substantiate, the presumption is that you either misread the instructions, were naive in your judgments, or simply a "typical taxpayer" inattentive to the tax importance of records. Any suspicion of dishonesty by the auditor is uncalled for. The personal whims of an auditor are irrelevant.

Two. *You have the right of additional time for substantiation.*
If the auditor disallows an item because your records or documentation are inadequate, you can ask for more time. Request that he indicate alternative forms of substantiations that would be acceptable.

Three. *You have the right to an explanation of any disallowance.*

After considering your best substantiation of an item, and the auditor disallows it, you can request an explanation of his position. If necessary, you can request that he show you "the book" (laws, regulations, rules) on it. You cannot expect an extended educational discourse, but you are entitled to the gist and reference authority for his disallowance.

Four. *You have the right to limit the audit to the checked boxes only.*

As a taxpayer, you have the burden of verifying each and every item of deduction on your return. As an auditee, however, you have a right to limit the audit to those specific items checkboxed in your notification letter. This means that if the auditor branches out and expands the scope of the audit, after you have substantiated the boxes checked, you have cause for complaint.

Five. *You have the right to be treated courteously and reasonably.*

You are a taxpayer. You have the right to expect those in government to treat you as such. They are not your servants, but you are not theirs either. If an auditor starts making threats of any kind, or starts getting hostile and completely unreasonable, you have a right to *stop* the audit at that point. Fold up your files and records and leave.

Six. *You have the right to phone your Congressman's office . . . from the IRS.*

This is where that little card mentioned above, tucked in your pocket, comes in handy. As you prepare to leave the office of a hostile auditor, ask to use his phone. If he refuses, ask where his supervisor's office is. If he won't tell you, then ask another auditor nearby. Go to the supervisor's office and ask to use the phone. You have a right to call your Congressman's office while on government property: the IRS office. Tell the IRS supervisor that you want to complain about the auditor. Some supervisors may listen. Others may not.

When encountering a headstrong government agent, taxpayer rights become a matter of interpretation. Whose interpretation prevails — yours or his — depends on the fact and circumstances of each audit case. Nevertheless, you have the right to be treated courteously and reasonably, without vindictiveness or harassment. Section 7602, quoted in Chapter 1, does not authorize maltreatment of auditees.

Clarify Contradictory Positions

One situation that an auditor enjoys is when a taxpayer corners himself into a contradictory position. On one tack or the other, the auditor will prevail. A taxpayer (auditee) cannot have it both ways on the same tax issue.

A "contradictory position" occurs when a double benefit is taken for the same event, at different places on a tax return. For each event or class of events recognized for tax purposes, there can be only one benefit: not two. If an auditee has claimed two, he will lose one or the other. This is a cardinal rule in tax theory of long standing.

A simple illustration of contradiction is interest received versus interest paid. The rules require that all interest received be reported as income. There are no offsets. Interest paid out can only be deducted as mortgage interest on Schedule A or as business interest on Schedule C. Where Schedules A or C are not used, the desire is to reduce the amount of interest received by that which was paid out. Where either schedule is used, the tendency is to understate the interest income and simultaneously overstate the amount paid out. To most taxpayers, interest is interest: one form should be allowed to offset the other. These feelings lead to contradictory positions in reporting interest income and deducting interest outgo.

Another example is state income tax. The amount of such tax withheld and/or paid during the year is deductible on Schedule A. However, if there is a state tax refund, the amount of refund is includible as income. This confuses many taxpayers; they feel that the refund inclusion (on Form 1040) is unfair. Nevertheless, a separate line on the income section of Form 1040 states—

Taxable refunds of state and local income taxes (do not enter an amount unless you deducted those taxes in an earlier year).

So, if one deducted state and local income taxes on Schedule A in a prior year, any refund of those taxes is includible as income.

A very common contradictory situation is where married taxpayers file separate returns. The higher income spouse takes all the personal deductions on Schedule A, whereas the lower income spouse claims the standard deduction. This is a flat "No-No." If one spouse filing separately itemizes deductions, the other must itemize. If one takes the standard deduction, the other must do so. The spouse filing first sets the stage for the subsequent-filing spouse.

Based on these examples, every auditee owes it to himself to go through his return with a fine-tooth comb. He should seek to identify every contradictory position that he may have taken. Upon doing so, he should clarify his position so that he can insist on whichever is most tax beneficial to him. He should do this well before his first appointment in the audit process.

Winning Is Not 100%

Winning an audit is pretty much like a sporting event. Rarely is one side 100% victor and the other side 100% loser. In most cases, the winner has a higher score than the loser. The score could be 10 to 9, 10 to 5, 10 to 1, or some other. Even the winner loses a point now and then.

And so it is with a tax audit. Rarely does one side score 100% and the other side 0%. Even where there is no additional tax due, the auditee may lose a point or two before the final tax is determined. It is totally unrealistic to go into an audit with the expectation that an IRS auditor will lose 100% on every issue raised. Most auditors are more experienced in audit matters than are taxpayers.

Therefore, winning an audit does not mean 100% victory. Winning means that one's additional tax to pay, if any, is *less than* the hourly quota (performance standard) set for the audit staff as a whole. As mentioned previously, the audit quota is believed to be between $300 and $500 in additional taxes per hour. We stress again that this is an estimate and a belief only. We have no inside track into the IRS performance standards staff.

For illustration purposes, let us assume that the acceptable performance quota is $300 per hour. That is, on the average, all auditors in a group must produce $300 or more per hour of audit time. Suppose in your case, after two hours with an IRS auditor, you had to pay $150 in additional tax. You have clearly won your audit!

The auditor should have gotten $600 or more from you (for two hours) but instead got only $150. This means that he has a $450 deficiency ($600 minus $150) in his "quota bank." He has to make this up from some other auditee. If he does not do so by the end of the performance review period, he may not get the salary increase that he or she had hoped for.

Consequently, winning an audit is a matter of keeping the additional tax below $300 per audit hour. If all auditees could do this — which is most unlikely — the IRS would have a hard time justifying to Congress why its audit staff was so large. The IRS might even take a second look at its DIF formulations.

In some cases, an auditee may come out with either a "no change" (meaning no additional tax) or "additional refund" (meaning a refund in excess of that sought when filing his return). In these cases, the auditee is a 100% winner. Since every auditee cannot expect to do this well, he can still be a winner if his additional tax is less than the hourly audit performance standard.

The Magic of Good Preparation

Most taxpayers lose an audit for one simple reason: preparation. Either they are poorly prepared, or they do not know how to prepare. Good preparation for an audit truly works magic.

Good preparation works magic because when an auditor sees that you are well prepared, and that you can substantiate the principal issues raised, he is not going to waste his time undercutting his quota bank. He is going to turn you loose as soon as he can to catch the next auditee who is not prepared.

Here is a specific actual example that took place recently in the IRS office at San Jose, California. The taxpayer/auditee was a shoe salesman on a straight commission basis. All of his business travel and entertainment expenses were borne by himself. For the year under audit, his total expenses amounted to nearly $18,000. He was notified to substantiate these, line-by-line as they appeared on Form 2106: Employee Business Expenses.

Without explaining all of the preparatory tasks at this time (this is what the subsequent chapters are all about), he spent a good 20 hours in preparation. He got everything in order. He separated his expenses into specific categories: food, lodging, air fares, laundry, tips, car rental, phone calls, supplies, exhibit fees, drinks, and so on. He tallied each category with an adding machine tape. Behind each tape he had his customer appointment book, lunch diary, restaurant receipts, lodging bills, car rental statements, credit card charges, and so on. He was loaded for bear.

The IRS auditor assigned to the case was allowed three hours by his supervisor. In addition, the supervisor assigned two trainees to observe the audit process. The supervisor assessed the case as a potential $4,500 additional tax, thus storing up excess quota points at $1,500 per hour. Salesmen, generally, are regarded as snap auditees: poor record keepers.

Come audit day. The shoe salesman and his tax representative appeared. Within 15 minutes the auditor looked up and said: "The District Director is not going to like this." He winked at the tax rep.

Five minutes later the auditor said: "There is no point in our continuing. You have everything in order. I will put through a 'No-change' report. Goodbye."

Scheduled to last three hours, the matter was closed in 20 minutes!

The taxpayer, of course, was overwhelmed by his audit success. Then he began to wonder if all of his preparation time was worth it. After all, he spent 20 hours preparing for something that lasted only 20 minutes. "Was this a good deal?" he wondered.

Well, let us analyze it.

The taxpayer (married) was in the 28% tax bracket, after all business deductions. If he went into the audit cold, he stood to lose $18,000 in business expenses, This would have jumped him to the 33% tax bracket. His additional tax would have been about $6,000. Thus, for the 20 hours of preparation, he "earned" nearly $300 per hour ($6,000 ÷ 20 hours). As a top salesman, he netted (after expenses) about $60 per hour in shoe sales work. So, he definitely came out ahead.

As so can you . . . if you knuckle down and get prepared before going to your audit appointment.

4

DOCUMENT PREPARATION

Good Preparation For Audit Is A "Must" If One Wants To Pay Little Or No Additional Tax. Good Preparation Starts With Knowing One's Audit Year And Gathering All Documentation Applicable. "Gathering" Includes Third-Party Records, Cancelled Checks, Itemized Invoices, Acquisition And Disposition Statements, Capital Adjustments, Photographs And Sketches, Mileage Logs, Expense Diaries, And Declaratory Documents. It Is Better To Postpone An Audit Than To Go Poorly Prepared.

Winning your audit starts with good preparation for audit. Good preparation means getting all documents and papers in order, *prior to* your first appointment. The audit process is much like other experiences in life: first impressions tend to be more lasting.

One does not go to the audit appointment with expectation that the auditor will give detailed instructions on preparation for the audit. Each auditee must do the preparation himself/herself. It is better to postpone an audit (but no more than twice) than to be poorly prepared at the first appointment.

In this chapter we want to discuss general procedures for getting prepared for audit. We will do this without any specific issue or issues in mind. There are approximately 3,000,000 individual tax returns audited each year. Without introductory generalizations, it is impossible to treat each and every audit issue that could possibly arise.

Discount the Fairy Tales

As stated previously, about 3% of all individual tax returns are audited each year. Because of this relatively low percentage, certain myths and fairy tales emerge concerning audits. The tales balloon in response to the natural apprehension that audits engender.

Auditees who have been through the mill, if half successful, often embellish and exaggerate their experiences to the uninitiated. Pretty soon, taxpayers who have not (yet) been selected for audit begin to believe the stories they hear. Inwardly, they prepare for the time when they too might be audited.

Today, certain fairy tales seem to persist concerning how to win an audit. These tales are premised on techniques for "psyching-out" an auditor, and getting him (or her) to give up the examination effort. Don't *you* count on it!

One technique is to appear at the audit appointment with several shoe boxes full of receipts and papers. At the opportune moment, one takes the shoe boxes and turns them upside down, dumping a huge pile of papers on the auditor's desk. The auditee then says, "Everything is here that you asked for; I've got to get back to work." As the story goes, the auditor starts into the pile of papers, but soon gives up in exasperation. He closes the case and calls the auditee to come pick up his papers.

Another technique is to appear at the appointment with a tape recorder. The recorder is brought in a briefcase, together with a few of the audit papers requested. After introductory courtesies, the auditee pulls out the tape recorder, sets it up in front of the auditor and turns it on. This is supposed to put the auditor on notice. Some auditees rely on this technique as a form of intimidation under the guise of taxpayer rights. It rarely ever works. The auditor simply puts his hand over the sound pickup, and tells the auditee either to turn it off or get permission from the District Director before recording.

Still another technique is the "money value" argument. The auditee comes in with one audit issue reasonably well documented. As the auditor examines the document, the auditee engages him in a discussion of the value of paper money. The auditee takes a dollar bill out of his pocket and points to the illuminated eye over the pyramid. When the auditor starts looking at it, the auditee launches into a discourse on the fraudulence of Federal Reserve Notes. "They are not backed up by real money such as gold and silver," he tells the auditor. Pretty soon — the story goes — the auditor's quota time is used up. He rushes to close the matter favorable to the taxpayer.

Be forewarned. The techniques above and others comparable will *not* work. IRS auditors are specifically trained to be alert for all techniques designed to dissuade them from their tasks. They have developed a standard procedure for response. The end result is to treat the auditee as being in default, and to assess him additional tax accordingly.

The only psyching technique that will work — if you want to refer to it as such — is to be well prepared with the right document(s) in direct response to each issue that the auditor raises. Once an auditor sees that you are prepared to substantiate each and every point that he raises, he will close the audit. Not because you have psyched him out of it, but because he does not want to run up unnecessary performance deficiencies in his quota bank.

Recordkeeping Is Required

Back in Chapter 1 we quoted the basic authority for the IRS to examine (audit) individual tax returns. That was Section 7602 of the Internal Revenue Code. The key phrase therein pertinent here is—

The Secretary is authorized . . . to examine any books, papers, records, or other data which may be relevant or material to such [audit].

Some auditees want to argue that this examination power is an invasion of their privacy, and is in violation of their constitutional rights. Amendment 4 (searches and seizure) and Amendment 5 (self-incrimination) are frequently cited as bases for objections to audits. These constitutional rights, however, apply to criminal investigations only. They do not apply to civil tax audits. Many, many federal courts have so ruled.

A civil audit is beyond the reach of constitutional avoidance. It is beyond reach for the reason that Congress has enacted a specific statute requiring that tax records be kept, and that these records be made available to IRS examiners. The specific statute on point is Section 6001: *Notice of Regulations Requiring Records, Statements, and Special Returns*.

The portion of Section 6001 pertinent here is—

Every person liable for any tax imposed by this title [Title 26: Internal Revenue Code], . . . *shall keep such records, render such statements, make such returns, and comply with such rules and regulations as the Secretary . . . deems sufficient to show whether or not such person is liable for tax under this title.*

The "regulations" to which Section 6001 refers is Regulation 301.6001-1. It reads in full as—

For provisions requiring records, statements, and special returns, see the regulations relating to the particular tax.

In other words, the type and kind of records required will depend on each tax issue and on each audit issue. No specific kind of records will serve all audit purposes.

What the above means is that books and records *shall be kept* on each item entered on each individual's own tax return. Furthermore, the records must be of a documentary form that is clear and complete with respect to an entry item. Vague and partial records are unacceptable.

There are no formal specifications as to what records are to be kept, or how they are to be kept. The only statutory phrase used is "sufficient to show whether or not one is liable for tax" on a particular transaction or event. This implies a consistent record-keeping practice: organized and self-explanatory.

It does not matter that one's books and records are kept in a crude or unorthodox manner. Mere erasures, inaccuracies, and strike-overs will not render records invalid. They are "sufficient" as long as they correctly reflect income, deductions, credits, allowances, expenses, and other items shown on an income tax return. The IRS cannot impose recordkeeping standards other than that they be of substance, be timely prepared, and be bona fide. This leaves much to the innovation and ingenuity of each auditee.

Know Your Audit Year

One innovation to good documentary preparation is to know your audit year. Tax audits are usually conducted two, three, or more years after a return has been prepared and filed. During the interim, many taxpayers truly have forgotten what took place in the year under audit. Many who otherwise keep good current records, cannot find their records several years later. In the ordinary course of living, records become separated and stored in different places. And the years are often mixed and commingled, and become indistinguishable.

If one is being audited for 1998, for example, records for 1996 or 1997 will do no good. Neither will records for 1999 or 2000. If 1998 is your audit year, you must gather forth and corral only those documents which are valid for 1998. A valid document is one which is applicable to a payment made in the year under audit. This means any time on January 1 through December 31 of the audit year. Documents dated December 31 are particularly scrutinized.

Many persons keep all kinds of records, many of which, unfortunately, have no bearing on an audit issue. They search through these in an aimless manner, hoping to find the magic one to satisfy the auditor. In doing so, they start reading and recalling events that are unrelated to the issue(s) under audit. They not only clutter their minds with nonaudit matters, they confuse themselves as to which year is which. They get rattled and become unable to focus on the year in question.

A typical example of the year-confusion that arises pertains to property tax statements. Every local taxing authority issues each year a property tax bill on all real property within its jurisdiction. Most statements are on a fiscal year basis, assessed in two installments. All local property taxes paid are deductible on appropriate federal schedules. Confusion arises as to which installment is deductible in which federal year.

Take the state of California, for example. Property is assessed on March 1 of each year, at a tax rate effective for the fiscal year commencing July 1. The first installment is due on December 10, and the second is due April 10. Most taxpayers pay on time. Two or three years after the payments are made, there is utter chaos in determining the amounts paid in the federal year under audit. If you do not believe this, take a look at Figure 4.1

Figure 4.1 shows two local fiscal years spanning the federal audit year 1998. Note that there are *four* installment dates. Can you select the two applicable for federal 1998?

Answer: 2nd installment 1997-1998 due April 10, 1998, and 1st installment 1998-99 due December 10, 1998.

There are many other documentary examples of confusion as to the applicable year. A doctor's bill or a mortgage statement may be rendered for December 1998 and be paid in January 1999. If 1998 is the audit year, is the 1999 payment valid? The answer is "No."

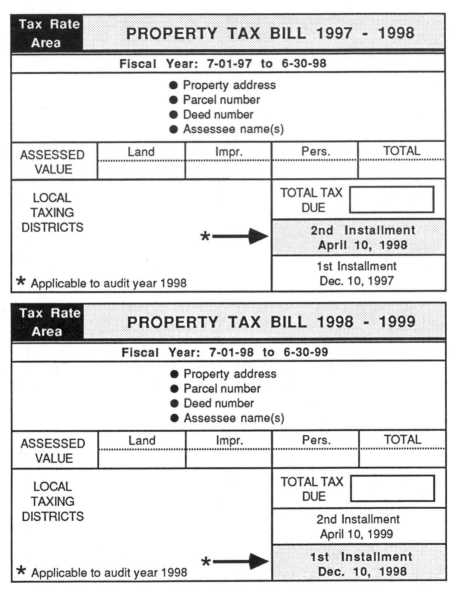

Fig. 4.1 - Example of Year-Confusion with Fiscal Documents

There is only one point being made above. It is that the very first step in preparing good documentation for audit is to *know thy audit year*. Be ruthless in eliminating or setting aside any and all papers that are not strictly applicable to the year under audit. It is no use trying to argue why a document should be applicable, or was intended to be, or should have been.

Third-Party Documents

One of the best verifications of an item on a tax return is a third-party document. In every audit issue there are two adversary interests: the auditee (individual taxpayer) and the auditor (government agent). Thus, a "third party" is a person or entity who is neither auditee nor auditor. A third-party prepares his document unaware of, and unconcerned with, whether an audit takes place or not. He does so in the ordinary course of business.

Since the third party is not involved in the audit, the presumption is that the facts and circumstances reported (on the document) are indeed correct. The document becomes prima facie evidence of the truthfulness and accuracy of a fact or payment. If a third-party document is directly applicable to an audit issue, and is presented timely by an auditee, the auditor has the burden of disproving it or justifying its nonacceptability.

The convincing feature of a third-party document is that it is prepared at the time a transaction or event takes place, or is a summary of all events within a specified calendar period: day, month, year. It is not "doctored" after the fact to beat an audit issue.

What are some third-party documents acceptable on their face by IRS auditors?

A good first example is a payment statement on one's mortgage or other loan(s) against one's home. Most banks, savings and loans, and mortgage companies furnish debtors with periodic statements on the status of their loan(s). Although a total payment is made, the receipt is broken down into the portion applied to principal, the portion applied to interest, and the portion applied to taxes (real estate).

Another example is a confirmation statement prepared by a mutual fund or stock brokerage firm. Such a statement identifies the type of transaction (buy, sell, exchange), the dollar amount involved, the price per share, the number of shares transacted, and a share balance or dollar balance, as appropriate. There is also a year-to-date summary of dividends and distributions paid.

Another example is a purchase order or disclosure statement. If one buys a car, for example, he is given a copy of the purchase agreement therewith. It describes the car and its accessories; it lists the purchase price, the sales tax, and license fee. It also gives information on insurance coverage, installment payments, rate of interest, and so on.

Another example is a medical bill submitted by doctors and hospitals. The bill states the amount of charge(s), amount(s) paid on account, adjustment(s), if any, and the balance due (if any). The bill also shows an "explanation of charges" either by a code number, letter symbol, or checkbox. The manner of payment (cash, check, money order, or insurance reimbursement) is also shown.

Still other examples are cash receipts issued by retail businesses such as restaurants, food stores, hardware stores, repair shops, and the like. These documents usually show the service or product sold, its unit price, its extended price, and other related information. They are prepared on the spot without any audit consequences in mind.

The most acceptable third-party documents are those in preprinted form showing the name of the entity (trade, business, or profession), with the name of the debtor (auditee) typed or handwritten thereon. The date of preparation must be shown, together with specific date or dates of payment credits. It is a document dealing with *one class* of items only, or describing one single transaction.

A recap of three forms of third-party documents almost always accepted by an auditor is presented in Figure 4.2. Every auditee should do his best to support his tax return entries with *directly applicable* third-party documents.

Cancelled Checks

One shortcoming with third-party documents is that the date-of-payment credit is not always clear and specific. Sometimes a payment is made by a debtor near the end of the year, or after the due date shown on the statement. The debtor is then credited in the following year or in the following billing period. This creates audit uncertainty. Any uncertainty is justification for the auditor not to accept the third-party document.

In cases like this, the third-party document must be backed up by a cancelled check (personal, money order, or cashier's) signed by the auditee. A **cancelled check** — if identifiable with and applicable to a specific audit issue — **constitutes one's "bare bones" proof of payment**. The date that the check is written is clearly shown thereon; the signature of the payer is clearly shown

MORTGAGE STATEMENT

	LENDING INSTITUTION
Loan No._____	
Mortgagee _(name, address)_	Date___(prepared)___
	Year-to-Date
Date paid_____	
Amount paid_____	Interest paid_____
To principal_____	Taxes paid_____
To interest_____	Principal bal._____

MEDICAL BILL

	MEDICAL ASSOCIATION
Patient____(name, address)	
	Adjustments_____
Date of service_____	Bal. due_____
Type of service_____	
Service charge_____	Explanation of Service:
Previous bal._____	☐ ☐
Amount paid_____	☐ ☐
Date paid_____	☐ ☐

AUTO PURCHASE

	AUTO COMPANY
Stock No._____	
Purchaser_(name,address)	Date of Purchase_____
Base price_____	Description of Trade-in:
Accessories_____	
Total price_____	
Sales tax_____	Statement of Insurance:
Warranties_____	
License fee_____	Credit Application:
Cash price_____	
Trade-in_____	Proceeds of Loan:
Cash down_____	
Unpaid bal._____	Security Interest:
Finance chg._____	
No. of payments_____	Service Contract:
Total to pay_____	

Fig. 4.2 - Facts Presented on Acceptable Third-Party Documents

thereon; and the name of the financial institution on which the check is drawn is preprinted thereon. The date of cancellation of the check, while not always clear and legible, is proof certain that the check went through the system and was handled by persons unknown to the checkwriter.

As a simple example of the audit importance of a cancelled check, consider payment made to a doctor or hospital on December 31, 1998. Chances are it would not be credited to one's account until, perhaps, January 15, 1999. If 1998 is the year under audit, only the cancelled check will satisfy the auditor that payment was made in 1998, if indeed it was mailed on December 31.

How can an auditor tell if a check was mailed on the date entered on its face?

He flips the check over and scrutinizes the cancellation stamps thereon. Sometimes there are as many as three or four such stamps, depending on the banking industry procedures. If the earliest cancellation stamp is within three business days of December 31, the presumption is that the check was timely mailed. Allowing three days for mailing and handling a check forecloses the possibility of writing a check on December 31, then holding it a week or two before mailing.

Another use of a cancelled check is to prove who actually made the payment. Rarely does a third-party document indicate who actually made the payment. An auditee's account may be credited, yet the payment may be made by someone not under audit. This situation arises frequently between parents and adult children, and between co-owners of property.

For example, consider that two persons A and B (who are not spouses) own jointly a piece of rental income property. They share expenses on an informal basis. In 1998 owner B pays the property taxes, but owner A is under audit. Owner A furnishes a cancelled check to the auditor. The auditor immediately notes that owner B signed the check. Will he allow the amount as an expense deduction on owner A's tax return?

Generally not.

If owners A and B have a joint checking account, and can prove that they do, the auditor will allow it. He will also allow it if there is a *written agreement* between the two owners that they will share the expenses interchangeably on a specific fractional basis. Otherwise, an auditee gets no credit on his tax return for expenses paid by a taxpayer not under audit.

Cancelled checks constitute primary evidence in controversial audit issues such as alimony, child support, property settlements, casualty losses, breach of contracts, and other litigative matters.

We cannot overstress the importance of cancelled checks in tax audits. This fact alone pretty well rules out ever achieving a 100% plastic money (credit card) society. Credit cards and credit institution billings are virtually worthless for audit purposes.

Electronic Statement Problems

The marvel of computer technology in the modern-day business world cannot be denied. All kinds of financial transactions can be conducted with electronic speed. Exchanges between accounts, credits and debits, and crisp descriptive codes, all are taken care of in the flick of a key touch. Everything is so "user friendly."

But a truly major system flaw prevails. Electronic statements are NOT TAX AUDIT FRIENDLY.

Although IRS auditors use computers themselves, they will not automatically accept other computer statements as prima facie evidence of fact. Other "hard evidence" is needed.

Perhaps two recent examples (actual audit cases) will make the point.

A 60-year-old taxpayer was engaged in extensive commodities transactions. In the process, he suffered $235,000 in trading losses. He properly claimed these losses on Form 6781: Gains and Losses From Contracts and Straddles. Upon audit, the monthly electronic statements (12 in all) were submitted. The auditor reviewed these statements and, arithmetically, verified the cumulative amount of loss. However, he wanted more positive proof that the taxpayer indeed had put up $235,000 of his own money.

The taxpayer's brokerage firm was contacted. After several weeks, the brokerage firm supplied 55 pages of electronic statements with color coded references to numerous bank wire transfers from other accounts. The sum total of the bank transfers matched the $235,000 figure above. Still, the auditor was not convinced that the money was not created out of electronic thin air. He wanted the original bank deposit slips!

The taxpayer/auditee had numerous investment accounts over the prior 25 years. There was no way in the world he could resurrect the original bank deposit slips. Even if he could, the figures would not correlate with those above. The auditor and auditee were at an impasse. Finally, the auditor accepted the brokerage reports.

On another audit occasion, the taxpayer had claimed $6,500 in legitimate business expenses. He had five credit cards at the time and used them interchangeably for business and personal expenditures. He kept all of the monthly statements and marked those items which were business. He had authorized his bank to make automatic payments to the creditors. Consequently, he had no first-hand evidence of payment other than the electronic statements. In this particular case, the auditor disallowed the entire $6,500.

Both of these examples point up the fact that electronic statements alone, even though totally of third-party origin, are not always accepted as conclusive evidence of payment. Most auditors want to see a cancelled check or other direct receipt for every deduction claimed.

Invoices and Itemizations

The shortcomings of cancelled checks is that they do not always (on their face) identify what was paid for. A check is filled out *Pay to the order of*, but this does not adequately describe the nature of the payment. In many audit situations, the name of the payee is not self-explanatory in terms of audit acceptability.

Let us illustrate this situation with contrasting examples.

A taxpayer (auditee) is in the equipment rental business with an office and repair shop. He gets a monthly phone bill which he pays by check. The check is made payable to the Abalone Telephone Company. If the company is not engaged in services other than telephone communications, the "pay to" on the cancelled check is quite self-explanatory.

On the other hand, suppose a cancelled check was made payable to the Modern Design Company. And suppose the amount was for $1,633. No auditor, no matter how reasonable and cooperative, could possibly know what the $1,633 is for. Invariably, he will ask to see a billing invoice or other itemized statement describing the $1,633.

Suppose the invoicing letterhead of Modern Design Company included subheadings such as Repairs, Remodeling, Construction: Commercial/Industrial. What would the $1,633 be? Would it be an expense item (repairs) or would it be a capital item (remodeling and construction)? An auditor could not tell.

To determine the proper allowance, an auditor would have to examine some invoice or statement allocating the $1,633 to various items. Suppose the statement reads as follows:

Painting of office............................	$ 338
Remodeling of shop........................	816
Installing work benches....................	479
	$1,633

Now, what does the auditor do?

He allows $338 for painting the office as a current business expense. Remodeling the shop and installing work benches — total of $1,295 (816 + 479) — are allowed as a capital cost. Capital costs, however, cannot be expensed in the year of occurrence. They must be amortized over the useful life of the expenditure, say 10 years in this case.

From the foregoing, it should be obvious that invoices and itemizations become important documentary evidence in certain tax-fact situations. In many cases, applicable invoices and statements do not indicate payment credits. Nevertheless, they explain what was paid for when other payment evidence is submitted.

To be acceptable for audit explanation, the invoices and itemizations must be timely prepared. This means within normal business practices, which is usually 30 days. Short descriptions are acceptable so long as the name and location of the invoicee (auditee) are clearly indicated.

For audit purposes, invoices and itemizations need not be formal, nor on any preprinted format. Stamped headings and handwritten entries on plain paper may be used. They may even be prepared by the auditee himself. However, they must be authenticated by entry of amounts by the invoicer (third party), with a signature or initial near the bottom line.

Acquisitions and Dispositions

Property acquired for use in a trade or business, or for investment, is a capital asset. During the period of holding by an auditee, the property may experience certain transformations and allowances. It may be improved, altered, damaged, or reconstructed; it may be subject to allowances for depreciation, depletion, energy credits, conservation benefits, and so on. When the property is disposed of (by sale, exchange, or otherwise), a capital accounting is required. This accounting is called *cost or other basis as adjusted*.

The "cost or other basis" is a tax reference for determining the amount of gain or loss on the disposition. There may be capital gain or ordinary gain; there may be capital loss or ordinary loss. Much depends on the nature of the property (real, tangible, intangible, or personal) and on its use during the holding period. Different tax rules apply for capital versus ordinary, and gain versus loss.

Where a number of different rules apply to a taxable disposition, an auditor wants to see the whole history of events. He wants a complete documentary trail from date of acquisition to date of disposition, including any and all intermediate adjustments. He wants to satisfy himself that the adjusted capital basis used by the auditee is correct. After this verification, he then wants to be satisfied that gain or loss is characterized properly as capital, ordinary, or a combination thereof.

When the acquisition and disposition are a year or so apart, with no owner-induced changes in between, the documentary history is quite simple. The auditee gathers his "buy" document and matches it with his "sell" document. The difference is a gain or loss. Stock transactions through a brokerage firm are an example of this sell-buy matching.

But let the time-lapse between acquisition and disposition be 10 years or so, with multiple intermediate transformations and allowances, and the documentation trail becomes a major audit preparation problem.

Most auditees do not keep a good documentary trail of capital assets held more than two or three years. It's all a "pain in the neck," they complain. As a result, formal records (third party) get lost or misplaced; informal records become incomplete or unspecific.

To illustrate the typical documentary inadequacies involved, let us consider an auditee who bought a twin-engine airplane which he leased to a private flying club. As a new member of the club, he bought the airplane from a retiring member for $20,000. The "papers" on it, however, showed only $15,000. The $5,000 difference was a barter credit for sales tax, property tax, tie down fees, engine overhaul, federal inspection, and so on.

The buyer (auditee) leased the plane to his flying club annually, for a total of seven years. During this time he took accelerated depreciation on his income tax returns. During this time also, he had two major overhauls which improved significantly the useful life of the plane. One of the overhauls was necessitated by a crash, for which he was insurance reimbursed handsomely. After seven years, he sold the plane to another club member. He sold it for $15,000 with papers showing $12,000.

What documentation does our auditor need?

We are not going to answer this question here. To do so would take an entire chapter. The type of documentation required and its information detail will be discussed in Chapter 6: Cost or Other Basis.

The point above is that no single piece of documentation will suffice. Not even two documents (buy and sell) will suffice. For every capital aspect involved, a suitable document is needed. This includes the barter arrangement, overhaul, insurance recovery, depreciation, and other improvements. Things *can* get complicated.

Photographs and Sketches

Many auditees overlook the documentation value of photographs and sketches. They do so because they think a "document" has to be some kind of receipt for dollars paid. There are a number of situations where receipts alone are inadequate.

Consider, for example, an auditee who has rental property on a lake shorefront. The winter storms come and wipe out a portion of his property. To continue renting the property for income, the storm damage has to be repaired. In the process, he installs special storm structures to prevent similar damage happening again. He writes all of the costs off as a casualty loss. Two years after the casualty restoration, he is audited. What documentation does he need?

Cost receipts alone would not do. Most auditors would treat such receipts as evidence of capital improvements. Improvements cannot be current expensed; they must be amortized over the life of the structures. Thus, no casualty loss would be allowed.

In this case, photographs and newspaper clippings will be needed. Preferably, some of the photographs should be taken before the storm, some immediately after it, and some at each major phase of the restoration. Accompanying newspaper articles and photographs of the storm area add conviction to its occurrence.

Auditors, by nature and training, have very poor insight and imagination. Dollar figures on documentation are seen as cold black or cold white. There is no translative comprehension or association of these figures with a casualty in which the auditor's own property is not at stake. When chronologically presented with photographs, even the most hard-nosed auditor can be convinced.

Let us take another situation. An auditee has a 10-room house in which he lives and rents rooms to others. He allows his tenants to use certain common areas of the dwelling, such as the kitchen, family room, and so on. He reports the rental income and claims all expenses and depreciation on his dwelling. What documentation does he need?

In addition to receipts, he needs diagrammatic sketches and fractional computations. He needs a plan-view sketch of his total dwelling, approximately to scale. He needs to show the dimensions of his rented rooms, and the dimensions of the common areas. He also needs to show the dimensions of the space that, as owner, he uses exclusively, as well as space he uses in common with his tenants.

When all of the sketching is done, he needs to compute the percentage of the total dwelling that he uses on his own, and the percentage that the tenants use. Only the rental percentage can be applied to total expenses and depreciation base. This is called *allocation documentation*.

An illustration of the type of allocation sketch required is presented in Figure 4.3. Note that each area is indicated by its lineal dimensions and square footage. (The sketch is not to scale.) The different use areas are shaded. The net rental fraction is shown supported with computations.

There is no way in the world that receipts alone will satisfy an auditor for a situation such as in Figure 4.3. Appropriate sketches are absolutely necessary. They can be prepared by the auditee or by a professional.

Mileage and Expense Diaries

Many auditees are in an occupation for which they incur expenses that are tax deductible. They use their own car for business purposes and they spend small amounts out of pocket. Sometimes they are reimbursed by their employer or by their business, and sometimes not. Getting receipts for these expenditures is awkward and impractical. Even credit cards are unhandy, as not every vendor will accept them.

The only practical documentation in these cases is a mileage log and expense diary, prepared by the auditee himself. Such "documents" are quite acceptable if prepared *at or near the time of expenditure*. This acceptability is covered by Regulation 1.274-5T(c)(2).

Specifically, Regulation 1.274-5T(c)(2) accepts an auditee's diary for each entry less than $75. For greater amounts, there must be receipt backups, especially for lodging and air fares.

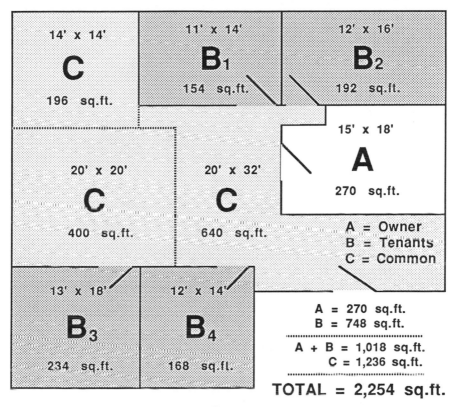

Rental space = $B + C (\frac{B}{A+B})$ = 748 + 908 = 1,656 sq.ft.

Rental fraction = Rental space / Total space = 73.47%

Fig. 4.3 - Measurement of Space : Rental Allocation

In the words of the regulation itself, a diary entry of less than $75 ($25 if expended before October 1, 1995) is acceptable if—

. . . it includes sufficient information to establish the amount, date, place, and the essential character of the expenditure.

We should hasten to point out now that Regulation 1.274 consists of 125 *separate* subregulations. These deal mostly with business expenses and travel and entertainment. These kinds of deductions are guaranteed audit targets, if any are claimed on your return. If you claim business travel, you'd better have a lodging receipt showing date, place, and amount.

A mileage log lists the date, place, purpose, and distance to and from a business visit. A "business visit" is that which is strictly in pursuit of one's trade, business, or profession. It includes a social element, such as entertainment, where the primary purpose is business motivated. A mileage log accompanied by a territorial road map constitutes near perfect documentation under the regulations above.

An expense diary must list the date, place, and purpose, but also must include the name or names of the business entity or person(s) involved. Listed separately are such items as meals (breakfast, lunch, dinner, snacks), drinks, lodging, laundry, public phone, parking, air fares, taxis, car rentals, fees, tips, small gifts, supplies, small tools, and so on.

In the situations above, the tax regulations are quite strict. The problem is that many auditees are just plain lazy. They want the tax benefits of the business deductions without the tedium of keeping daily records and diaries. Audit success in this regard is a matter of self-discipline and self-conditioning.

A summary of the determination required when preparing for audit is presented in Figure 4.4. It is — or should be — evident therein that you cannot get all of your applicable documentation ready in five minutes. You need adequate time to apply yourself methodically . . . and persistently.

Self-Serving Declarations

Auditors are given a limited degree of discretion on what they can allow solely on testimony of the auditee. If an auditee has presented good documentation on basic issues, sometimes his word alone will be accepted on supporting issues. This "sometimes" is a big unknown for one's preparatory effort. One should not rely too heavily on his word alone being accepted.

There are situations for which there is no plausible excuse for the absence of documentation. If an auditee has been negligent and inattentive to his recordkeeping duties, he should expect no mercy. If the dollar amounts are relatively small, it would be better to concede. Do not plead on testimony alone for small amounts. Let the auditor score a point or two.

On the other hand, there may be bona fide situations where there *is* a plausible explanation why no documentation exists. In such

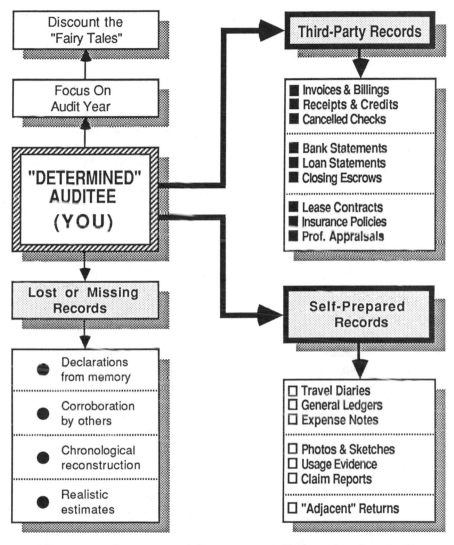

Fig. 4.4 - Summary of Documentary Preparation for Audit

event, an auditee's declaration under "penalties of perjury" can be — and usually will be — accepted.

An example would be the barter arrangement in the aircraft illustration previously discussed. A self-serving declaration by the auditee explaining the barter terms, and listing an agreed amount for each item bartered, plus other factual information unembellished, is generally acceptable. Particularly so if signed as being "true, correct, and complete" . . . to the best of one's knowledge and belief.

There are other situations considered unimportant or irrelevant at the time of expenditure. These, too, can be resurrected by declaratory documentation.

For example, consider two persons as close friends who together buy a piece of vacation property and subsequently fix it up. Because of different income levels, and available funds and time, they enter into no written agreement. They play it by ear, spending and fixing as they go along. Some years later the property is sold. They verbally agree to an arbitrary split of the profits. One of the seller's returns is audited. How does he establish his cost or other basis? He has no documentation whatsoever.

Here is where a notarized declaration comes in handy. The auditee prepares a Declaration of Contributory Interest in Property (or other suitable heading). He gives a brief description of the property, its location, its date of acquisition, and the arrangement that he and his friend had. Then he lists chronologically *each and every item* of his contributory interest: the amount of money he spent and the fair market value of materials and equipment that he supplied. He displays a bottom line total in dollars. His friend reads, verifies, and concurs in the total indicated. Together they go to a notary public and sign under oath.

There are two precautions with declaratory documentation. One, the declaration must be prepared *before* the first appointment in the audit process. It is presented in a timely manner with full expectation of its acceptance. Coming in with a declaration after an audit is well underway is too defensive in nature. No self-respecting auditor would accept an after-the-fact document.

The second precaution is: no more than one declaration per audit year. Rarely would an auditor accept more than one declaration, and only then for good cause. Declaratory documentation is not a crutch to be abused. We all learn from hindsight. If honest documentary omissions have been made, select the one that is most tax beneficial. No auditee should expect an auditor to accept a whole slate of self-serving declarations to match each audit issue raised. After all, the purpose of an audit is to verify entries on a return by documentation considered customarily proper.

5

INCOME VERIFICATION

In A Thorough Audit, The First Step Is A Determination Of One's Gross Income. This Includes All Income Derived From Personal Services, Business Profits, And Investment Risks. Where Income Is Not Reported By Payers Directly To IRS, 6 Income Reconstruction Methods Are Authorized. Bank Deposits Accounting Is Effective Against Skeptical Auditors. One Is Cautioned Against Omissions Of Income In Excess Of 25% Of His Reported Gross. "Understatement Of Tax" Is A Redefinition Of Income.

In Chapter 2, we listed certain payer forms on which income was reported directly to the Internal Revenue Service. These payer forms are grouped into three series, namely:

Series W-2: salaries, wages, bonuses, etc.
Series 1099: fees, commissions, rents, etc.
Series K-1: partnerships, trusts, etc.

Since these are third-party documents, they are accepted as prima facie evidence of the true amount of income paid. Except for obvious errors, these forms constitute full and adequate verification of the applicable income paid to a taxpayer/auditee.

There are, however, many income situations for which no payer forms are ever made — nor could be made. For example, no one is required to report fees paid to attorneys, doctors, general contractors, stock brokers, realty agents, consultants, and so on.

No one ever reports money paid to auto mechanics, house painters, laundry machine operators, barbers, coin dealers, bookmakers, insurance agents, hardware merchants, travel agents, or sidewalk venders. Payments to these and other persons and entities vary drastically in amount and regularity. It would be totally impractical to require clients and customers to report on IRS forms every dollar paid to tradesmen, professionals, and businesses.

Obviously, then, there must be some other procedure for verifying the gross income of an auditee, where W-2s, 1099s and K-1s are not applicable. There are such procedures, and we will discuss them below. But first we must explain what is meant by "gross income."

Gross Income Defined

In any really thorough audit, the first step in determining the correct tax is a determination of the correct gross income. The correct gross income consists of all income from whatever source derived, and in whatever form realized, be it money, property, or services. By self-definition, "whatever source" and "whatever form" mean all tax reportable income which is not specifically excluded by Congressional statutes. Taxable income is arrived at by subtracting allowable deductions from gross income.

Gross income is an all-sweeping concept. It springs directly from Amendment 16 of the U.S. Constitution. This amendment, repeated here, reads in full as follows—

The Congress shall have power to lay and collect taxes on incomes, from whatever source derived, without apportionment among the several states, and without regard to any census or enumeration.

With this broad grant of dictatorial authority, Congress quickly enacted Section 61(a) of the Internal Revenue Code. This section reads in full as follows—

Except as otherwise provided in this subtitle [Income Taxes], *gross income means all income from whatever source derived, including (but not limited to) the following items:*
(1) Compensation for services, including fees, commissions, fringe benefits, and similar items;
(2) Gross income derived from business;

(3)   Gains derived from dealings in property;
(4)   Interest;
(5)   Rents;
(6)   Royalties;
(7)   Dividends;
(8)   Alimony and separate maintenance payments;
(9)   Annuities;
(10) Income from life insurance and endowments;
(11) Pensions;
(12) Income from discharge of indebtedness;
(13) Distributive share of partnership gross income;
(14) Income in respect of a decedent; and
(15) Income from an interest in an estate or trust.

Note above particularly the phrase *including but not limited to*. These are dangerous words. They can be — and often are — interpreted by government agents to mean anything and everything . . . of money and value.

Restated in nonstatutory language, gross income includes all forms of compensation for personal services. This includes wages, salaries, commissions, fees, tips, bonuses, fringe benefits, severance pay, rewards, prizes, expense reimbursements, alimony, annuities, pensions, honorariums, unemployment benefits, gambling winnings, jury fees — any and all conceivable forms of compensation for services.

Gross income also includes profits and losses from proprietorships, partnerships, farming rentals, investments, and capital outlays for loans, property, and equipment.

If one is a U.S. citizen or a U.S. resident (whether citizen or not), his gross income includes sources throughout the world! One cannot avoid the income tax reportability burden by transferring capital or property outside of the territorial jurisdiction of the United States. Big Brother is ever alert for transactions involving money, property, or services over $10,000 to or from foreign jurisdictions. On gross income matters, U.S. sovereignty is **worldwide**.

In essence, the concept of "gross income" is a bold contradiction to our cherished constitutional freedoms. It is an extraconstitutional anomaly which has yet to be addressed in popular democratic fashion. It is an all-sweeping dictatorial concept. As a result, IRS auditors are trained to sniff out all possible sources of income which are not required reporting on Forms W-2, 1099, and K-1. In some cases, auditor imaginations can run wild.

Items Specifically Excluded

Despite the all-sweeping definition of gross income above, there are specific items of income which are statutorily excluded. The exclusions stem from the phrase in Section 61(a): "Except as otherwise provided."

It is important for every auditee to know — and master — the statutory exclusions from gross income. The reason is that even when omitted sources of income are not suspected, a routine introductory audit question is:

"Do you have any sources of income which you have not reported?" If you answer "No," the follow-on question becomes:

"Do you have any sources of income which you believe are nontaxable?"

Almost everyone has some nontaxable income, whether he realizes it or not. Some auditees report nontaxable income when it should not have been reported. Others fail to report income which they believe is nontaxable, but which in fact is taxable. There is much fear and confusion surrounding what is taxable and nontaxable gross income.

A very common example of this confusion has to do with disability payments. If the payments are made as a direct consequence of personal injuries or sickness due to—

(a)   workmen's compensation acts,
(b)   damage awards from lawsuits,
(c)   employer paid insurance plans,
(d)   active duty in armed forces, or
(e)   terrorist attacks on government employees,

then such payments are "specifically excluded" from gross income [Sec. 104(a)]. On the other hand, if one is a disabled retiree, he must be "permanently and totally disabled," and, if so, all of his disability income is includible, but he gets a limited offset in the form of a small credit against his taxes [Sec. 22(a)].

There are many of these maybe nontaxable, maybe taxable income situations. This is the underlying reason why auditors are trained to routinely ask about unreported sources of income. It is not that they necessarily suspect deliberate omissions: they know that the tax laws on nontaxable income are tricky and misleading. If you don't know what is nontaxable, auditors will trick you into reporting it anyway . . . because, often, they don't know either.

To clear the air on specific categories of income which are expressly excluded from gross income, Figure 5.1 is presented. The statutory reference for each exclusion is indicated, together with its thumbnail description. For most sources listed in Figure 5.1, there are statutory limits to the amount that is excludable. Particulary note in Figure 5.1 that there are some 35 categories (!) of nontaxable income. There are still other sections of the tax code where *portions* of one's income are nontaxable.

We urge you to study Figure 5.1 carefully. It may trigger some ideas of income which you have reported previously, and need not have reported. More importantly, it will give you confidence in stating what is not taxable, in response to an auditor's question concerning your gross income. It will be apparent below why this foreknowledge of nontaxable income is so important.

When Payer Forms Inapplicable

There are many occupations where payer reporting forms (W-2, 1099, and K-1 series) are totally inapplicable. We mentioned a few of these occupations earlier. Many others are self-evident. These occupations usually involve a trade, business, or profession where the principals are nonemployees. In these cases, an auditor has no other choice but to probe the gross income issue by whatever means and methods he can.

As a general rule, when an auditee's income derives from sources that constitute more than 25% of his payer-reported income, he can expect very penetrating income verification techniques.

To illustrate when to expect these techniques, consider a taxpayer whose payer-reported income is $40,000. On the side, he has a little business selling baby furniture out of his home. He incurs legitimate selling expenses. He grosses $3,500 from his sales and nets $1,500. The $3,500 gross income from his side business is less than 25% ($40,000 x 25% = $10,000) of his third-party reported income. If he keeps good records on his $3,500 gross sales, chances are the records alone will be audit-accepted (after casual examination).

But, suppose the figures are reversed. That is, a taxpayer/auditee has $3,500 in payer-reported income, and $40,000 from a trade or business. There are no third-party records whatsoever on the $40,000. Can an auditor be satisfied that the $40,000 is correct, just on the auditee's self-records and testimony alone? Not likely.

ITEMS OF INCOME NOT SUBJECT TO TAX

	ITEM	TAX CODE	AMOUNT NONTAXABLE
1.	Child support payments (re divorce)	Sec. 71(c)	As fixed by divorce decree or child support order
2.	Certain annuity proceeds	Sec. 72(b)	"Exclusion ratio"; investment divided by expected return
3.	Employee achievement awards	Sec. 74(c)	Up to $1,600 per year; see Sec. 274(j)(2)
4.	Employer paid group life insurance	Sec. 79(a)	Premium cost up to $50,000 coverage
5.	Social Security benefits received	Sec. 86(a), Sec. 86(c)	All if AGI less than $25,000 (s) / 32,000(m);otherwise, 50% Tier 1 taxable: 85% Tier 2 taxable
6.	Life insurance proceeds upon death	Sec.101(a)	All if premiums paid by taxpayer
		Sec.101(b)	Premiums only, if paid by others
7.	Gifts and inheritances	Sec.102(a) Sec.102(b)	All of principal and corpus; any income from property is taxed
8.	Interest on municipal bonds	Sec.103(a)	All "public activity" bonds; private activity bonds AMT taxed
9.	Compensation for injuries or sickness	Sec.104(a)	Workmen's comp.,personal injury awards, military disabilities
10.	Employer-paid group-term health plans	Sec.105(b)	Amounts actually expended for medical care, etc.
		Sec.105(c)	Loss of limb or disfigurement
11.	Employer contributions to health plans	Sec.106	All such contributions on behalf of the employee
12.	Rental value of parsonages	Sec.107	Clergymen only; to the extent actually used for home or rental
13.	Income from discharge of indebtedness	Sec.108(a)	Amount discharged in bankruptcy / insolvency; reduced by "tax attributes"
14.	Combat pay of Armed Forces	Sec.112(a)	Enlisted: all exempt
		Sec.112(b)	Commissioned: $500 / month
		Sec.112(d	Prisoners & MIA's: all exempt
15.	Scholarships and fellowship grants	Sec.117(a)	To the extent used for tuition & books & supplies
		Sec.117(d)	Reduced tuition for employees
16.	Meals or lodging for "convenience" of employer	Sec.119(a)	To the extent provided on "business premises" and camps
17.	Qualified group legal plans	Sec.120(a)	Up to $70 premiums per employee
18.	Sale of residence [old] after 5/6/97 [new]	Sec.121(b) Sec.121(b)	Up to $125,000 (if over 55) Up to $500,000 (any age)

Fig. 5.1 - Statutory Exclusions from Gross Income (continued)

ITEMS OF INCOME NOT SUBJECT TO TAX

	ITEM	TAX CODE	AMOUNT NONTAXABLE
19.	Certain uniformed services retired pay	Sec.122	Reduction for survivor's benefits and allocable consideration paid
20.	Insurance recovery: living expenses re casualty	Sec.123	To extent actually used for loss of occupancy due to casualty or disaster
21.	Cash in lieu of benefit plans	Sec.125	When choice of 2 or more qualified plans; employer premium equivalent
22.	Certain conservation subsidy payments	Sec.126	As certified by Secretary of Agriculture; not chargeable to capital account
23.	Educational assistance programs	Sec.127(a)	When employer sponsored, up to $5,250 per year
24.	Dependent care assistance programs	Sec.129(a)	When employer sponsored, up to $5,000 or earned income of employee
25.	Personal injury liability assignments	Sec.130(a)	To the extent of any qualified funding arrangement
26.	Foster care payments to care provider	Sec.131	Amounts up to 10 foster children under age 19; otherwise, up to 5 foster children
27.	Certain fringe benefits	Sec.132(a)	As defined by subsecs.(b),(c), (d), and (e); employer provided
28.	Certain military benefits	Sec.134	Any "qualified" allowance or in-kind benefit
29.	"Higher education" income from U.S.Savings Bonds	Sec.135(a) Sec.135(b)	Phase out applies to AGI's exceeding $40,000/$60,000
30.	Energy conservation subsidies	Sec.136(a) Sec.136(c)	Any "energy property" provided to customers by a public utility
31.	Cash or deferred arrangements	Sec.401(k)	Limited contributions to employer sponsored plans
32.	Foreign earned income & housing expenses	Sec.911(b) Sec.911(c)	Up to $80,000 on a "daily basis" Housing costs exceeding 16% of salary
33.	Recovery of "cost or other basis" in property sold	Sec.1011(a)	As per Sec.1012 (any property) and Sec.1013 (inventory)
34.	Property acquired from a decedent	Sec.1014(a)	Its fair market value at date of death
35.	Gain on small business stock	Sec.1202(a)	50% of gain from sale/exchange of stock held over 5 years

Fig. 5.1 - Statutory Exclusions from Gross Income (concluded)

The auditor needs more positive verification that the income is not $50,000 . . . or $85,000 . . . or some other imaginary figure.

An auditor cannot arbitrarily disregard an auditee's income records, just because he is curious, suspicious, or unconvinced that they are complete and accurate. If the records are kept in the ordinary course of the auditee's trade or business, and adequately reflect the income received, the auditor must accept them at face value. The "adequate reflection of income," however, must be customary and consistent. This includes daily income ledgers, weekly adding machine tapes, and monthly summaries with year-to-date accumulations. There must be a single — and chronological — set of books.

If an auditee's income accounting is habitually inconsistent, showing manifest errors and omissions, the auditor can disregard the records. He then has the prerogative of reconstructing the gross income by after-the-fact methods.

On what authority can an auditor disregard a taxpayer's income records?

In part, on the basis of Section 7602, presented previously in Chapter 1. And in part on Section 446(b): *Exceptions for Methods of Accounting*. Section 446(b) reads in full as:

If no method of accounting has been regularly used by the taxpayer, or if the method used does not clearly reflect income, the computation of taxable income shall be made under such method as, in the opinion of the Secretary, does clearly reflect income.

Needless to say, Section 446(b) has been tested many times in court. The most forthright judicial decision favoring the IRS is the *Holland* case: (1954) 348 US 121. In that case, the Supreme Court stated—

To protect the revenue from those who do not "render true accounts," the Government must be free to use all legal evidence available to it in determining whether the story told by the taxpayer's books accurately reflects his financial history.

Thus, an IRS auditor's authority to reconstruct income is clear. If an auditee's records are *inadequate* or *manifestly inaccurate*, the auditor can compute the auditee's gross income from whatever evidence is available.

Income Reconstruction Methods

Any of at least six different methods can be used by the IRS for reconstructing an auditee's income. These six different methods are:

1. Bank deposits
2. Application of funds
3. Percentage markups
4. Unit and volume estimates
5. Third party interviews
6. Net worth computation

Bear in mind that these are income *reconstruction* methods only. They are not everyday accepted accounting practices. At best, they establish approximations of income. They are acceptable as the "best evidence" of income, where a taxpayer's records can be shown to be inadequate. In every case, however, the IRS-reconstructed income will far exceed the true income. This is the risk you take for not keeping good income records.

Method 1

Under the bank deposits method, it is presumed that all deposits in financial institutions during the audit year are taxable income. Exceptions are those deposits which can be specifically identified as being nonincome or nontaxable. The burden of establishing this identity is on the auditee. The term "financial institutions" includes banks, savings and loans, money market funds, stock brokerage firms, credit unions, trust accounts, and the like, where deposits are made and third-party recorded.

Method 2

Under the application of funds method, the auditee's lifestyle and spending habits are scrutinized. His total expenditures for the year are determined. This includes expenditures for food, clothing, housing, furniture, autos, travel, entertainment, business, education, and so on. Then his documented cash on hand at beginning of year, plus reported taxable income, are subtracted from his total expenditures. The excess expenditures are presumed to be unreported taxable income.

Method 3

Under the percentage markup method, taxable income is presumed to be a percentage of some benchmark reference on the auditee's return. The reference may be gross sales, gross receipts, cost of goods sold, commissions paid, interest paid, accounts receivable, inventory on hand, accounts payable, and so on. Audited tax returns of those in a similar trade or business, in the same geographic area, with comparable experience, are used for establishing an average markup percentage. This "industry average," as it were, is then applied to the verifiable benchmark on the auditee's return.

Method 4

Under the unit and volume method, an estimate is made of the total number of units bought or sold, or total volume of transactions made for the taxable year. The basic ingredient of the auditee's trade or business is used for actual observational measurements by the auditor. For example, a hamburger vendor uses meat, a massage parlor uses towels, a bookmaker uses pari-mutuel tracks, a garage mechanic services cars. The auditor himself counts and measures these items during the normal course of business of the auditee. A sample period of time is selected, industry averages are applied, and taxable income is computed.

Method 5

Under the third-party interviews method, the auditor issues a summons for the customer, supplier, and/or client lists of the auditee. He then interviews these persons and establishes how much money each paid to the auditee, or how much money the auditee paid to them. An average customer/client day and an average supplier month are established. The annual gross dollars in and gross dollars out become a matter of extended arithmetic.

Method 6

Under the net worth method, the presumption is that any increase in net worth during the audit year is taxable income. Determining such an increase, however, requires establishing a *beginning* net worth with reasonable certainty. Thereafter, all assets and liabilities are scrutinized meticulously. Plus adjustments are made for nondeductible living expenses (estimated from government cost-of-living standards). Minus adjustments are made for nontaxable receipts such as gifts, bequests, insurance proceeds, capital gain deductions, and others specifically identified. Frequently, this involves income reconstruction over three to five years, whereupon an average is used for the audit year.

The net worth method constitutes the most comprehensive interrogation and analysis of all the reconstruction methods. Ordinarily it is employed only where willful evasion or substantial omission of income are suspected.

When Records Lost, Destroyed

It is not uncommon for an auditee to keep proper income records for tax preparation purposes, but when audit time comes, the records truly have been lost, stolen, or destroyed. If an audit were conducted on the very day of submitting a tax return, lost records would never present a problem. Unfortunately, audits lag the submission of a return by 18 to 36 months. During this interim, many events can occur beyond an auditee's control.

There can be fire, flood, earthquake, tornado, or other bona fide casualty to ravage and destroy one's tax records. There can be theft and vandalism of those records. Some other government agency or legal adversary can subpoena — and retain — the records for issues unrelated to federal taxation. Or, in moving from one place of business to another, the records may be inadvertently lost, misplaced, or damaged.

When an audit comes, any explanation that one's income records were lost, stolen, or destroyed is viewed with much skepticism. Most auditors do not have the capability to translate the misfortunes of an auditee into reasonable accommodation to the facts and circumstances. Said auditors resort coldly to Section 6001 (previously presented) which requires that records be kept. No extenuating circumstances are accepted.

Now, what does the auditee do?

For one thing, if he has been audited before, and his records then were found in good order, he can offer this as a basis for tempering the auditor's automatic suspicion of negligence or evasion.

On another tack, the auditee can prepare a declaration of the facts and circumstances surrounding the loss, theft, or destruction. The declaration (appropriately notarized) must describe the specific events involved, and any and all attempts made to resurrect the records. The reasons for inability of complete resurrection should be stated.

Partially resurrected records, where the income portions are missing, are sometimes worse than no records at all. This is particularly true if income records are missing while expense records are complete. In theft cases and lawsuits, this indeed could be the case. Yet the impression is that the auditee is playing games.

In the final analysis, there is a respectable course of action for the "lost records" auditee. He can use any of the above described six methods for reconstructing his income. He can pick one method for one year, and another method for another year. He cannot mix the methods for a given audit year. He cannot use the methods for ongoing accounting purposes, but he can use them in those situations where his records have indeed been lost, stolen, or destroyed.

Bank Deposits of Income

An innovative method for substantiating the gross income of nonemployee-type auditees uses bank deposits accounting. This is a form of recordkeeping which takes advantage of third-party, proof-positive aspects of banking procedures. Instead of waiting to reconstruct income this way, one deliberately employs his bank records as his income records. Much simplicity and positive verification can be achieved. Any auditor skepticism concerning other forms of income records is up-front washed away.

In most above-board businesses, statements, billings, and invoices are paid by personal check, money order, or credit card. Most payers prefer some kind of bank documentation for their payments instead of using greenback cash. They want cancelled-check type receipts for their own tax records, family budgets, and insurance claims. This fact can be incorporated into an auditee's income records, by simply depositing all payments made to him, and using the bank certification of the deposits as his third-party documentation.

To engage in bank deposits recordkeeping successfully, there must be *two* separate checking accounts: one for business use and one for personal use. The business account is the sole and exclusive depository for gross income from a trade, business, or profession. This presumes that all such deposits are not payer-reported to the

IRS. The business checking account accommodates no other sources of income, such as nontaxable and payer-reported (W-2, 1099, K-1) income. With strict self-discipline in this regard, there are no audit-haggling issues. All deposits made are taxable gross income (period!).

The personal checking account, on the other hand, accommodates three kinds of deposits. There are (a) transfer deposits, (b) nontaxable deposits, and (c) payer-reported deposits. The *transfer deposits* are transfers from the business account to the personal account. If clearly so identified, they cannot be taxed a second time.

The personal checking account is used for personal living expenses and passive investments unrelated to the business account. The only deposits in such accounts that are taxable are the payer-reported deposits. Since the IRS gets the originals of all W-2s, 1099s, and K-1s, auditors are not likely to deposit-haggle over these matters. Although not sacrosanct, the personal account is thus better isolated from audit attack.

A schematic diagram of the bank deposits arrangement for gross income records is presented in Figure 5.2. Note that the gross taxable income of the auditee consists of two parts: the unreported payer deposits and payer-reported deposits. This is much more convincing to an auditor than pages, books, and volumes of income records which list names, dates, addresses, and amounts paid by indvidual payers. Such records could be "manipulaed" if an auditee chose to do so.

Also note in Figure 5.2 that auditee deposits into interest bearing accounts, dividend paying accounts, and capital gain accounts are completely isolated from the business checking account. Nevertheless, most auditors — because their official instructions require they do so — will demand to see the deposit records for all personal investment accounts. It is up to the auditee to develop his case that no payer amounts go directly into these accounts. All investment deposits originate from the personal checking account. Cancelled checks from the personal checking account should convince the most skeptical auditor.

Duplicate Deposit Problems

There is one serious problem when an auditor insists on a bank deposits analysis. All deposits — repeat: *all* deposits — in all accounts are regarded as income, unless established otherwise.

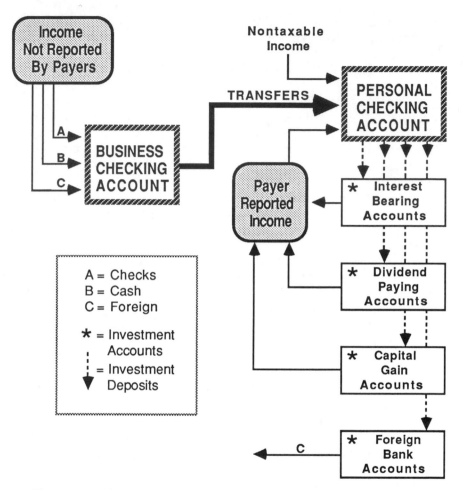

Fig. 5.2 - Disciplined Bank Deposits Accounting of Income

"Establishing otherwise" is the problem, particularly where there are duplicate deposits of the same money.

The problem is accentuated when there are multiple accounts involving indiscriminate transfers and rollovers. A "transfer" is money which has been deposited in one account in a taxable year, then transferred to another account (or accounts) in the same year. A "rollover" is money which has been deposited in one account, taken out, then subsequently redeposited again. Taxpayer/auditees tend to get careless about keeping track of their inter-account transfers and intra-account rollovers (especially in this electronic era). This carelessness can cause an auditor to assign a greater amount to gross income than is actually the case.

For example, if one deposits $100 in one account, then transfers it to three other accounts during the year, the auditor's worksheet will show $400 in deposits. It is up to the auditee to prove that only $100 — the first deposit — is tax accountable income. Establishing that the other three deposits are duplicates of the first is painful and frustrating. You know that they are, but how does the auditor know? You have to put a tracer on each deposit and prove the duplication. This often is difficult two, three, or four years after the deposits have been made.

A recent case on point will illustrate the agony that can be involved.

The taxpayer/auditee had a small business which grossed (approximatley) $300,000 for the year. This amount was the invoiced "accounts receivable" which he could identify. He deposited this money into his business checking account. Into the same account, however, he also deposited investment proceeds, savings transfers, closeout of personal accounts, insurance reimbursements, lines of credit, and employee tax withholdings. The auditor tallied up $735,000 in deposits: $435,000 more than his gross sales. Because of tracing problems with the electronic transfers, the $435,000 could not be positively identified. Consequently, the auditor asserted that the entire $735,000 was taxable gross income!

The message here is clear. Every deposit made must be *tax-character identified*.

Identify the characterization at the time of the deposit: not weeks, months, or years later. Keep a chronological file of each deposit slip, with your handwritten "trail notes" thereon. Do not lump deposits into one where more than one tax character is involved. Instead, make multiple deposits: each separately identified. Photocopy the necessary backup information and attach to your deposit slips.

Foreign Bank Accounts

Associated with Form 1040 (Individual Income Tax Return), there is a Schedule B. This schedule is titled: **Interest and Dividend Income**. It is arranged in three parts, namely:

Part I   —   Interest Income
Part II   —   Dividend Income
Part III   —   Foreign Accounts

It is Part III that upsets many auditees. They consider this as unwarranted invasion into their financial privacy.

Part III consists of two questions, "A" and "B," each of which is supposed to be answered "Yes" or "No." Question A pertains to individually owned foreign financial accounts; Question B pertains to interests in foreign trusts, partnerships, and corporations.

Question A reads as follows—

At any time during the tax year, did you have an interest in or a signature or other authority over a bank account, securities account, or other financial account in a foreign country? (See Instructions.) Yes_____ No_____.

In essence, the instructions say to check "No" if the combined value of the account was $10,000 or less during the whole year. Otherwise—

Get Form 90-22.1 to see if you are considered to have an interest in or signature or other authority over a financial account in a foreign country.

Form 90-22.1 is titled: Report of Foreign Bank and Financial Accounts. It is *not* a tax form and therefore, if applicable, is *not* to be filed with the IRS. It is a Treasury form to be sent directly to: Department of the Treasury, P.O. Box 32621, Detroit, MI 48232.

At the very bottom of the front page of Form 90-22.1 (small print), there is a section headed "Privacy Act Notification." Thereunder are the typical government threats of fine or imprisonment for failure to complete the form. The purpose of the form, it says, is—

for collecting information to assure maintenance of reports or records where such . . . have a high degree of usefulness in criminal, tax, or regulatory investigation or proceedings.

In other words, if you live in the U.S. and have any kind of foreign account, you are automatically suspected of laundering money or being a tax evader.

If you do have foreign sources of income, whether connected with your trade or business or not, deposit-report same in your business checking account as depicted in Figure 5.2. Treat such foreign income as not payer reported to the IRS (which is correct). Make any transfers to foreign accounts from your personal checking account. This way, you have cancelled checks to prove that you are not engaged in drug smuggling, mafia activities, investment swindles, or tax evasion. Then answer "No" to Question A.

Question B has to do with setting up and transferring money to foreign trusts. Again, if you derive income from such trusts, deposit-report same as above. Then answer "No" to Question B. After all, it is the *income* that they are after: not the manner and means for deriving it.

Avoid Substantial Omissions

Some auditees are genuinely irritated by the income tax system. They see the high salaries and benefits paid to government employees, the high tax-exempt expense accounts allowed legislators, the tax-free income paid to Federal Reserve Board members (Sec. 137(a)(5)), the high pensions and short weekdays of federal judges, and the billions of dollars of transfer payments to military contractors and foreign governments.

Many auditees deeply resent working their fannies off to pay taxes to support Big Government which is "harassing" them by selection for audit. As a result, sometimes such auditees are willing to take some risks and not report some of their income.

If one wants to take a risk in not reporting some of his income, that is his affair. This book is a "tax guide"; it is not a conscience guide nor a guide on philosophy. One's political and economic views are his own. But if he is going to take some risks, he should know the *danger threshold* . . . and heed it.

The danger threshold lies in what is called the "substantial omission" rule. This rule says, in effect, that if an amount of gross income in excess of 25% of the gross income shown on a taxpayer's return is omitted, the government (IRS) has six years to uncover the omission and collect additional tax . . . plus penalties . . . plus interest. The rule applies to income taxes, gift taxes, death taxes, and excise taxes.

As it relates to income taxes, the substantial omission rule is cast in concrete in Section 6501(e)(1)(A). This statute reads in relevant part as follows—

If the taxpayer omits from gross income an amount properly includible therein which is in excess of 25 percent of the amount of gross income stated in the return, the tax may be assessed, or a proceeding in court for the collection of such tax may be begun without assessment, at any time within 6 years after the return was filed.

(ii) In determining the amount omitted from gross income, there shall not be taken into account any amount which . . . is disclosed in the return, or in a statement attached to the return, in a manner adequate to apprise the Secretary of the nature and amount of such item.

In other words, "substantial omission" is statutorily defined as more than 25% of one's reported gross income. Included in the gross income is *any disclosure* on the return or its schedules, by which the nature and amount of omission can be ascertained by analysis and computation. A "disclosure" is the same as reporting the income, even though it is not part of one's own tax computation.

If an auditee wants to take a risk, he should be fully aware of Section 6501(e). That is, he should calculate his risk to be less than 25% of his reported gross income. If $1 more than 25%, he opens himself up to six consecutive years of audit!

If the less-than-25% risk fails, be prepared to concede the issue and pay the additional tax. There is no acceptable basis for omitting income unless it is genuinely believed to be nontaxable. (Recall Figure 5.1.)

Understatement of Tax

Recently, the concept of gross income, as defined by Section 61(a), has been redefined. Congress — with prodding from the IRS — has come up with a back-door approach called *"understatement* of tax." The focus is on the catch-word "understatement": not on underpayment, failure to report, or anything like that.

The theory of income understatement shifts into gear when an auditor disallows any deduction — any at all. When this happens, the taxable income is increased and, thereby, so is the tax. Taxable income can also be increased by an auditor altering depreciation schedules, valuation statements, cost or other basis, and generally any attributes on one's return that benefit the taxpayer.

The presumption is that one made these alleged "understatements" negligently, willfully, and with intentional disregard for the rules and regulations. Bona fide differences in opinion on the interpretation of tax laws, by decree, no longer exist.

Congress, in Section 6662(d)(1)(A) of the tax code, ruled out bona fide differences of interpretation, by defining "substantial" understatement as—

There is a substantial understatement of income tax for any taxable year if the amount of the understatement for the taxable year exceeds the greater of—

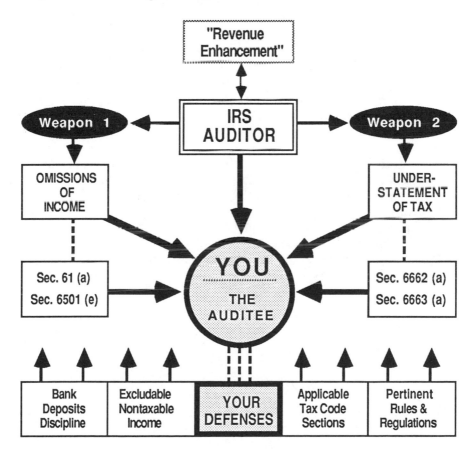

Fig. 5.3 - The "Silent Weapons" You Face in Every Audit

(i)   10 percent of the tax required to be shown on the return, or
(ii) $5,000.

The 10% or $5,000 is an unduly narrow limit of tolerance for human interpretational differences in complex tax laws. This narrow tolerance makes the IRS a virtual dictator on judgmental matters. Any auditor can easily disallow enough items to surpass the 10%-$5,000 threshold.

Once an auditor forces an understatement of tax by 10% or $5,000 or more, two penalties come automatically into play, namely:

1. the 20% accuracy-related penalty [Sec. 6662(a)], and
2. the 75% imposition of fraud penalty [Sec. 6663(a)].

The danger with these two penalties is that they are imposed without restraints . . . and without objective standards. The IRS can — and does — impose the penalties at whim. When this happens, the burden is on the taxpayer/auditee to prove *by a preponderance of evidence* that the penalties do not apply (Sec. 6663(b)). This turns our cherished principle of "innocent until proven guilty" completely on its head.

Before going on to the next chapter, we want to summarize the key elements of this chapter. It is not that we want to overdwell on the elements herein; it is just that we want you to be aware of the exposures that lie before you. We depict these exposures in Figure 5.3. The message being presented is that (I) omission(s) of income and (II) understatement(s) of tax are the "silent weapons" being used against you to garnishee additional revenue into federal coffers . . . without raising taxes(?).

6

COST OR OTHER BASIS

One Area In Which Many Auditees Are Inexperienced And Unknowledgeable Is "Capital Accounting." This Is A Trail Of Cost Or Other Basis Adjustments To Property From Date Of Acquisition To Date Of Disposition. Basis Adjustments, Particularly Depreciation, Are Longstanding Arguable Issues. Arguments Arise Because Of The "Allowed/Allowable" Theory. With This Two-Edged Theory, Current Deductions Are Minimized And Gains On Sales Are Maximized. Inventory Is "Locked-Up" Capital Until It Is Sold. The "Uniform Capitalization" Rules Of 2,500-Word Section 263A Are A Real Bear Trap.

The term "basis" is a tax accounting reference, with respect to which gains, losses, depreciation, amortization, inventory, and recovery computations are made. Basis is a *benchmark* which measures the amount of capital outlay for an asset at any point in time subsequent to its acquisition. Hence, the proper basis in an asset is a prerequisite for determining the correct tax allowances (if any) therewith.

Basis is fundamentally an accounting for one's capital outlay in an asset, be it tangible, intangible, real, or personal. The capital outlay may be in the form of money (cash or check), debt obligation (loan), property (trade or exchange), or service (barter). No matter how an asset is acquired, the collective term that describes its capital basis is: *cost or other basis, as adjusted.*

It is this "as adjusted" feature that IRS auditors count on for meeting their performance quota and/or for creating understatement-of-tax income.

Many auditees are quite unfamiliar with capital accounting. They confuse it with expense accounting. They pay out X-number of dollars in a given year, and they want an X-dollar deduction in that year. The extent of deduction allowed or allowable depends on the nature of the asset acquired, and on its subsequent use. Property assets used in a trade or business are capital accounted for differently from assets acquired for investment or for personal use.

Capital accounting and expense accounting are as different as night and day. If an item has been expensed on a return when it should have been capitalized, the result invariably will be additional tax for the expensed year. Winning an audit in this case becomes more difficult. It is not so much a matter of documentary preparation as it is a clear knowledge of capital (basis) accounting rules.

Capital vs. Expense Items

Let us illustrate the difference in tax treatment between a capital item and an expense item. To do so, let us assume that our auditee made a $5,000 expenditure during the tax year. For introductory simplicity, assume that it was a cash outlay evidenced by a cancelled check and a descriptive invoice.

If the $5,000 transaction is for the acquisition of a capital item, it *cannot* be written off in full in the year of expenditure. Depending on its nature and use, the writeoff may be "stretched out" over the useful or recovery life of the asset.

If the $5,000 transaction is an expense item, it can be written off in full in the year of expenditure.

Can you not sense the immediate difference in audit-year tax benefits for a capital versus expense item? The capital writeoffs are less beneficial than expense writeoffs. This is why an auditor will look into an auditee's capital accounting procedures with a fine tooth comb.

Suppose the $5,000 expended was for mortgage interest on the auditee's personal residence. This clearly is an expense item: fully deductible in the year paid. If in a trade or business, and the $5,000 was paid for commissions, insurance, repairs, or other operating expense, it, too, would be fully deductible.

Suppose the $5,000 was the base price for the purchase of a family auto. Does one get a tax writeoff for this? The answer is "No." Tangible assets acquired for exclusively personal use enjoy no tax writeoffs whatsoever.

Now suppose the $5,000 was paid for a parcel of raw land, or for the purchase of mutual fund shares. These are clearly investments. Does one get any writeoff? "No." But, if later either investment was sold for $6,000, one gets his $5,000 back at no tax, and pays tax only on the $1,000 gain.

Another suppose: the $5,000 was paid for a piece of machinery or equipment used in a trade or business. Does one get any tax writeoff? "Yes" . . . some.

If it were classed as 5-year equipment, one would get at least $1,000 tax writeoff each year. One might get more than, or less than, this amount, depending on his depreciation/recovery options and on when it was placed in service: early year, mid-year, or end of year.

Instead of being held for five years, suppose the equipment was traded in for another piece of equipment after three years. Does one get his full $5,000 writeoff then? "No," he does not. He starts a new depreciation/recovery schedule with the new equipment "adjusted" for the book value (unrecovered cost) of the old equipment traded in.

Now do you see why every cash outlay — no matter how well documented — is not an automatic tax writeoff in the year of expenditure? The nature of the expenditure determines whether it is an expense item (current-year writeoff), or no writeoff until sold, or a pro rata writeoff over the use period of the item acquired.

If an auditee goes into an audit without properly classifying his expenditures, he can be in for some surprises. Auditors just love to stretch out tax expenditures over as long a period of time as possible. This markedly ups their audit quota reserve.

Tax Schedules Affected

Auditors can raise capital basis issues on all of the primary schedules attached to an individual's tax return. These are Schedules A, B, C, D, E, and F. In addition, there are supplemental forms on which there may be basis issues.

For example, on Schedule A (Itemized Personal Deductions), the basis issues relate to property contributed to charitable organizations, and to casualty and theft losses. If noncash property is contributed to charity, Form 8283 is required (on which the term

"Donor's cost or adjusted basis" is used). If there is a casualty or theft, Form 4684 is required (on which the term "Cost or other basis in property" is used).

On Schedule B (Interest and Dividend Income), the basis issues are indirect. On Part II (Dividend Income), there may be nontaxable distributions. If so, these distributions become an adjustment (reduction) to basis of the dividend-paying stock, that, when sold, would appear on Schedule D (Capital Gains and Losses). On part III (Foreign Accounts), there may be transfers of property to foreign banks or foreign trusts. If so, Forms 926 and 3250 (for basis accounting) must be used. Form 926 uses the term "Cost or other basis," whereas Form 3250 uses "Value of property transferred and its adjusted basis." When the property transferred is sold, the transaction would appear on Schedule D, or on one or more supplements thereto.

The chief audit issues, however, arise primarily from "cost or other basis" entries on Schedules C, D, E, and F, and their supplemental forms. The titles of these schedules and forms are:

Schedule C	— Profit or (Loss) from Business
Schedule D	— Capital Gains and Losses
Schedule E	— Supplemental Income Schedule
Schedule F	— Farm Income and Expenses
Form 2106	— Employee Business Expenses
Form 2119	— Sale of Principal Residence
Form 4562	— Depreciation and Amortization
Form 4797	— Supplemental Gains and Losses
Form 4835	— Farm Rental (or Fishing) Income
Form 6252	— Computation of Installment Sale
Form 6781	— Gains and Losses From Contracts and Straddles

On every one of these schedules and forms, there is a line or column heading with the words "cost or other basis" (or variant thereof). The variants may be "depreciation, allowed or allowable," "cost of goods sold," "marked to market," or other. As an auditee, you must know the specific locations of these headings on the applicable forms attached to your own return. Then get prepared for the scrutiny ahead.

Even if every other entry on your tax return can be 100% substantiated, cost or other basis can still cause audit changes. One reason for difficulty (and possible change) is that, more often than not, cost or other basis data applies to, or should have applied to, one or more years *prior* to the audit year. Under these circumstances, cost or other basis documentation is an exception to the preparatory instructions given previously in Chapter 4. There, we were concerned with current expense items. Here we are concerned with capital cost items.

When a cost or other basis entry is subject to audit, the documentation required *starts* with the initial acquisition of the asset or assets involved. When there are multiple assets acquired over varying periods of time, corralling and organizing the documentation for audit can be quite painful. Particularly so if one has been cavalier and not kept a separate (cumulative) cost or other basis file. If the audit issue can be raised, you have no choice but to dig back and produce . . . or reconstruct.

Cost as Basis

The ordinary concept of "cost" is deceptive. What is treated as cost for tax purposes usually differs from what one ordinarily thinks of as cost. Tax cost is the amount paid for property in cash, promises, services, and other property. This includes all related costs to acquire legal title to property and to position it "on location" for the taxpayer's dominion and control.

The very first requirement of tax cost is that the property be acquired through an *arm's-length purchase*. The amount, form, and time of payment are irrelevant Whether the buyer paid more or less than it is worth elsewhere is not of tax concern. There is no adjustment to cost for good bargains or bad bargains, so long as the agreed price is above board between unrelated and unconniving seller and buyer. Pure economic and business considerations must prevail.

If property is bought on credit and/or with borrowed funds, cost is the full purchase price plus associated loan costs, other than interest. This includes loan application fees, "points" where customary, broker commissions, appraisal fees, title searches, credit checks, inspections, permits, freight, and so on. All costs of borrowing money and acquiring title are properly includible in initial cost basis, so long as there is full legal obligation on the acquirer to repay the borrowed funds.

If property is bought with other property traded in or other services rendered, the cost portion is one's basis in the property traded plus fair market value of the services rendered. Where traded property is involved, cost confusion arises because the value of property contributed and its basis may be, and often are, different. For example, a piece of business equipment traded in for another piece of equipment may have a market value of $3,000 with a basis of $2,000. The cost element in the transaction is $2,000 (not the $3,000 "value").

Cost does *not* include those portions of a purchase contract that can be properly written off as expense items, either in the year of acquisition or amortized over more than one year.

To illustrate the cost distinction for basis purposes, the itemizations in Figure 6.1 have been contrived. The listings in Figure 6.1 are representative of the kinds of information that appear on a purchase contract involving a piece of equipment used in a trade or business.

Assume that the data in Figure 6.1 is for five-year equipment. It was bought in 1996. Your tax return for 1998 is being audited. What is the cost basis that should appear on your return?

As you can see in Figure 6.1, cost is not the total price nor contract amount. It is a dollar figure somewhat lower. There are adjustments for expense items, amortized items, and basis transfer of property traded in. Now, perhaps, you can appreciate the importance of an acquisition document several years preceding the actual year under audit.

What happens if you cannot find, cannot resurrect, or cannot reconstruct such a document? The answer is simple. The auditor is instructed to assign you a "zero" cost basis. This automatically eliminates all tax benefits associated with cost.

"Other Basis" Explained

The term "cost" (or cost basis) applies strictly to assets acquired by first-hand purchase only. There are ways of acquiring assets other than by direct purchase.

There are acquisitions by exchange, acquisitions by gift, acquisitions by inheritance, acquisitions by distributions from a trust, partnership, or corporate entity; there are acquisitions by discharge of debt, acquisitions by involuntary conversion, and other forms of acquisition by transfer. Hence, the term "other basis" is used to accommodate those situations in which property is acquired other than by purchase.

Usually, there is much difficulty in establishing an audit-acceptable basis in property when not acquired by direct purchase.

EXAMPLE: NEW EQUIPMENT WITH WARRANTY & TRAINING CONTRACTS				
ITEM	AMOUNT	COST	EXPENSE	COMMENT
List Price	9,860	9,860		Capital
Accessories	1,720	1,720		Capital
Freight	850	850		Capital
Sales Tax	740	740		Capital
Inspection Permit	80	80		Capital
Warranty (3 yrs.)	1,000		333/yr.	Amortized
Insurance (2 yrs.)	900		450/yr.	Amortized
Training (6 mos.)	500		500	Less than 1 yr
TOTAL PRICE	15,650			
Less Credits				
Cash Down	3,500			
Trade-In Value	3,000	(1,000)		Adjustment
(Basis 2,000)				
BALANCE	9,150			
Plus Charges				
Credit Check	100	100		
Loan Fee	350		70/yr.	Amortized
Interest (5 yrs.)	3,430		686/yr.	Amortized
Loan Principal	9,150			
CONTRACT AMOUNT	13,030			
COST BASIS		12,350		
1st Yr. Expense			2,039	

Fig. 6.1 - Cost Extraction from Hypothetical Purchase Document

The reason for difficulty is that the auditor has to delve into the cost basis of the property in the hands of the owner preceding the taxpayer under audit. Prior owners of property, if accessible, are not very understanding or cooperative, when it comes to providing documentation on property they no longer own. Only when the prior owner has gone through the tax wringer in some way is there adequate documentation for the subsequent owner.

To illustrate the "other basis" audit-accounting problem consider a Section 1031 exchange. An exchange is the reciprocal transfer of "like kind" properties used in a trade or business, or for investment, or for the production of income.

Taxpayer A (now under audit) who formerly owned a parcel of land in County X, acquired by exchange a parcel of land in County Z, formerly owned by taxpayer B (not under audit). A's land had a market value of $35,000 with a cost basis of $10,000. B's land had a market value of $85,000 at time of the exchange. A paid to B $10,000 in cash, plus stock worth $20,000 (with a basis of $3,000), and machinery worth $20,000 (with a basis of $4,000). Taxpayer A paid $3,000 in exchange expenses. What is A's basis in property acquired from taxpayer B?

A's basis in the land acquired from B by exchange is the sum of the following:

1.	Basis in A's land given	$10,000
2.	Cash given	10,000
3.	Basis in stock given	3,000
4.	Basis in machinery given	4,000
5.	Exchange expenses paid	3,000
	Total	$30,000

In other words, A acquired a piece of property worth $85,000 for a basis of only $30,000. Since he did not purchase the property outright, he has no cost basis in it. Instead, he has an "other basis" as computed above.

In the exchange illustration cited, the acquisition basis rule is Section 1031(d). It reads in edited part as follows:

If property was acquired on an exchange . . . , then the basis shall be the same as that of the property exchanged . . . increased in the amount of any gain recognized [or cash paid . . . or other property transferred] *. . . decreased in the amount of money received* [including the relief of any debt liability].

There are many other rules for establishing the basis in property acquired other than by purchase. There are simply too many such rules to discuss here. A nearly complete listing — 30 in all — is presented in Figure 6.2. Figure 6.2 is a handy reference for the

INTERNAL REVENUE CODE	
Subtitle A - INCOME TAXES	
Chapter 1 - Normal Taxes and Surtaxes	
Subchapter C - Corporate Distributions and Adjustments	
Sec. 307	Basis of distributed stock and stock rights
Sec. 334	Basis of property received in liquidation
Sec. 358	Basis to distributees in reorganizations
Sec. 382	Loss limitations following ownership change
Subchapter K - Partners and Partnerships	
Sec. 722	Basis of contributing partner's interest
Sec. 723	Basis of property contributed to partnership
Sec. 732	Basis of distributed property other than money
Sec. 733	Basis of distributee partner's interest
Sec. 742	Basis of transferee partner's interest
Subchapter O - Gain or Loss on Disposition of Property	
Part II - Basis Rules of General Application	
Sec. 1011	Adjusted basis for gain or loss
Sec. 1012	Basis of property: cost
Sec. 1013	Basis of property included in inventory
Sec. 1014	Basis of property acquired from decedent
Sec. 1015	Basis of property acquired by gift
Sec. 1016	Adjustments to basis
Sec. 1017	Adjustment for discharge of indebtedness
Sec. 1019	Property involving leasehold improvements
Part III - Common Nontaxable Exchanges	
Sec. 1031	Exchanges of property for productive use
Sec. 1032	Exchange of stock for property
Sec. 1033	Involuntary conversions
Sec. 1034	Rollover of gain on sale of residence
Sec. 1035	Certain exchanges of insurance policies
Sec. 1036	Stock for stock of same corporation
Sec. 1037	Certain exchanges of U.S. obligations
Sec. 1038	Certain reacquisitions of real property
Sec. 1041	Transfers between spouses in divorce
Sec. 1042	Sales to employee stock ownership plans
Sec. 1044	Rollovers into specialized small businesses
Part IV - Special Basis Rules	
Sec. 1055	Redeemable ground rents
Sec. 1059	Reduction in basis for nontaxable dividends
Sec. 1060	Allocation rules for asset acquisitions

Fig. 6.2 - Reference Tax Code Sections for Basis Rules

auditee who wants to bone up on the basis rules affecting his property, prior to audit.

Adjustments to Basis

The cost or other basis above is one's initial or *acquisition* basis. Subsequent to acquisition, usually, there are adjustments to basis. There are "plus" adjustments and there are "minus" adjustments.

The plus adjustments are such things as improvements and additions which increase the cost or other basis. The minus adjustments are such things as insurance reimbursements and tax allowances (depreciation, deletion, amortization) which reduce the cost or other basis. The net result of all the pluses and minuses is an *adjusted* basis.

We have oversimplified, somewhat, the adjustments to basis. They are much more involved than we have indicated, The full range is detailed in Section 1016(a): *Adjustments to Basis*. The general rule thereof reads in introductory part as follows:

> *Proper adjustment in respect of the property shall in all cases be made —*
> *(1) for expenditures, receipts, losses, or other items, properly chargeable to capital account . . .*
> *(2) for exhaustion, wear and tear, obsolescence, amortization, and depletion to the extent* [allowed or allowable].

Within Section 1016 (shown as a single entry in Figure 6.2), there are some 30 statutory adjustments to basis. We have quoted only two immediately above. The others relate to land, buildings, structures, vehicles, machinery, equipment, stocks, bonds, contracts, debt relief, research expenses, personal residence, furniture and fixtures, capital recovery, and so on.

When one's cost or other basis in an asset is under audit, not only is the acquisition document pertinent, but so is documentation (or explanation or computation) for each and every adjustment made since acquisition. If one has held an asset 5, 10, 15, or more years before the audit, it is a formidable task to satisfy an auditor that you have followed the adjustment rules properly. The best way to convince him —if at all possible — is to be your own expert on the requirements of Section 1016.

All Adjustments Arguable

In the ordinary audit, no issue is more arguable than adjustments to basis. If an auditor cannot find anything else on a return to disallow, he will always fall back on adjustments to basis. This is known among tax professionals as an auditor's *quota safety net*. In 99% of the cases, an auditor can at least maintain his quota standard by attacking an auditee's cost or other basis. If an auditor does so aggressively, it is your cue that he has lost on every other point.

Why are adjustments to basis so arguable?

First of all, the rules for basis accounting (Figure 6.2) are unbelievably complex. They are subject to every interpretative whim of each auditor. Secondly, an auditor can bank on the reluctance of most auditees to take an unresolved adjustment into Tax Court. If an auditor's quota standard is $300 per hour, for example, and he makes a $325 adjustment, he knows that it will cost an auditee more than this to litigate the issue in Tax Court.

The great bulk of audit arguments over adjustments to basis have to do with depreciation. This is a statutory allowance addressed fully in Section 167 of the Code. The general introductory rule thereunder reads as—

There shall be allowed as a depreciation deduction a reasonable allowance for the exhaustion, wear and tear (including a reasonable allowance for obsolescence)—
(1) of property used in the trade or business, or
(2) of property held for the production of income.

The above reads simply enough. But what is "reasonable allowance"? Who determines it and how?

Altogether, Section 167 and its companion, Section 168, cite 18 different rules on reasonable allowance for depreciation!

Let us illustrate the arguable aspect with a very common, everyday, tax audit situation. The auditee has a piece of residential rental property which he bought three years ago for $65,000. The property was 40 years old when he bought it. He spent $10,000 remodeling it and another $6,000 for all new appliances. He has a 30-year first mortgage on the property, and a five-year "second" for the remodeling. He paid cash for the appliances. He intends to hold the property for five years, then sell it at a profit. What is a "reasonable allowance" for his depreciation deductions?

Immediately, any auditor would question the $65,000 purchase cost. He would require that this cost be allocated between land and building. (Land does not depreciate.) He would demand to see appraisals thereon by the local county assessor. Assume that the land is appraised at $30,000 and the building at $35,000. Hence, the auditee's depreciation base starts at $35,000: *not* the $65,000 that he paid for the property.

This miffs the auditee, but he accepts the auditor's assertions gentlemanly.

The next question that comes up is the useful life of the building. Chances are, the auditee will have used five years, because that is as long as he intends to keep the property. Therefore, he would have claimed $7,000 per year depreciation ($35,000 ÷ 5 years).

The auditor will say: "No. You've got a 30-year mortgage, so we'll use a 30-year life. This will give you a depreciation deduction of $1,167 per year ($35,000 ÷ 30 years) instead of your $7,000." (The less deduction, the higher the tax. Can't you see the setup?)

The auditee starts to argue, but he backs off, not knowing what is coming next.

For the $10,000 remodeling costs, the auditee would have written them off in five years. Using the auditor's mortgage life "decision" above, the five years seems reasonable, because that is the second mortgage life. Thus, the depreciation would be $2,000 per year ($10,000 ÷ 5 years). Or, would it?

"No, no," the auditor says. "The remodeling expenditures are part of the building structure, inseparable from it.. You must use 30 years. So, your depreciation is $333 per year ($10,000 ÷ 30 years).

The auditee starts to let it come out now. "Hey," he says. "You used the mortgage life on the $35,000, but you are not using it on the $10,000. How come? You can't have it both ways!"

"Oh yes, we can," the auditor beams. "We have a 'Revenue Ruling' on it. If you want to fight it, you'll have to go into Tax Court." (Revenue Rulings are one-sided dictates by the IRS itself. They are *not* judicial rulings. They are instructions to auditors, who cannot ignore them.)

Now that the auditor has the auditee on the run, the $6,000 for appliances is questioned. Since the auditee paid cash for them, he wrote them off in full in the year of purchase.

"No, no, no," the auditor says firmly. "Those appliances will last more than one year. Our guidelines say they will last six to eight years. I'll be reasonable with you and use six years. That will give you $1,000 per year in depreciation: not the $6,000 that you used."

By this time, if you are average taxpayer/auditee, you are ready to tear the auditor apart . . . and the whole Internal Revenue Service.

See what we mean?

When Assets Sold

When property other than inventory is sold (or otherwise transferred) it has an "adjusted basis" for determining the amount of gain or loss. The general rule in this regard is Section 1011(a): *Adjusted Basis for Determining Gain or Loss.*

Section 1011(a) reads in part as follows:

The adjusted basis for determining the gain or loss from the sale or other disposition of property, whenever acquired, shall be the basis [as per Figure 6.2] *. . . adjusted as provided in Section 1016.* [Emphasis added.]

Particularly note the phrase: "whenever acquired." This is your tip-off that, in an audit situation, there still can be considerable haggling over one's adjusted basis at time of sale. This time, however, the IRS switches its hat around and attacks the auditee from the other side of the coin.

Instead of trying to minimize the allowable deductions each year before sale (as discussed above), in the year of sale audit effort is made to maximize the adjustments. This comes under the administrative theory of *allowed or allowable*. This is a longstanding tax theory propounded in Revenue Rulings to IRS auditors.

The allowed/allowable theory is a two-sided weapon against an auditee. On the "allowed" side, an auditor seeks to minimize the deduction adjustments so as to maximize annual revenue: that is, before the year of sale of an asset. When an asset is sold, the "allowable" side is used: that is, the maximum allowances are arbitrarily assigned. This maximizes the gain (and minimizes the loss) so that, again, maximum revenue from the sale is derived. It is "heads you lose" and "tails . . . you also lose."

The two-sided allowed/allowable theory is small printed as: *Depreciation allowed or allowable since acquisition.* It is applied in the following sequence of gain/loss computational events:

Step 1 — Gross sales price
Step 2 — Expense of sale
Step 3 — Subtract Step 2 from Step 1
(net sales price)
Step 4 — Depreciation/Recovery
Allowed or Allowable
(since acquisition)
Step 5 — Cost or other basis
Step 6 — Improvements (since acquisition)
Step 7 — Add Step 5 and Step 6
Step 8 — IF GAIN
Step 3 plus Step 4, *minus* Step 7
Step 9 — IF LOSS
Step 7 *minus* Step 3 and Step 4

If Step 4 (allowed/allowable) is maximized, the resulting gain is also maximized. If a loss, with Step 4 maximized, the resulting loss is minimized. (Verify this with your own numbers.) In both cases, the tax revenues are enhanced. This is called the *theory of convenience* for government.

There is an important forewarning in the above. If the year of sale of property is under audit, the "since acquisition" procedures will apply. This means a detailed 9-step review of the cost or other basis history of the property involved. So be forewarned; prepare your case diligently.

Carefully — and meticulously — document Steps 1, 2, 4, 5, and 6. (Steps 3, 7, 8, and 9 are computational steps which follow from the documentation steps.) Then stand your ground against the allowed/allowable attacks. If appropriate, countercharge the auditor with asserting inconsistent positions. This sets the stage for a legitimate protest, if and when the need arises.

Cost of Goods Sold

Another cost item subject to attack during audit is cost of goods sold. The term "goods" refers to an *inventory* of merchandise or products held for sale to customers in the ordinary course of business. Unlike productive assets, inventory is not subject to depreciation, It is, however, subject to methodical accounting practices which an auditor needs to verify.

Inventory on hand at the end of the taxable year is locked-up capital. That is, one's investment in inventory just sits and sits . . .

until it is sold. There are no tax writeoffs or stretchouts whatsoever. Consequently, the temptation is to trim year-end inventories as much as possible so that some benefits can be derived from the money invested.

Trimming of inventory can be done by year-end sales, discarding of unsalable or damaged merchandise, gifting it away to charitable organizations, or by marking it down in value. The lower the year-end inventory, the higher the cost of goods sold, and the lower the tax consequences. Being aware of this, cost-of-goods auditors will dwell on your inventory accounting methods.

The simplest and safest inventory procedure is the cost method with physical inventory. Costs are set by supplier invoices which can be shown to the auditor. Taking physical inventory is tedious and time-consuming, which no auditor will do. However, if the inventory is taken and verified by a third-party (not the auditee), most auditors will accept it.

Sometimes the "cost" of inventory is adjusted for changes in market value. There may be changes in supplier prices, changes in market demand, and changes in the forces of inflation/deflation. Any adjustment to the original supplier cost must be substantiated with a consistent rationale from year to year. A key auditor question that is invariably asked is —

Was there any change in determining quantities, costs, or valuations between opening and closing inventory? ☐ *Yes;* ☐ *No. If "Yes," provide explanation.*

Other than beginning-ending inventory costing, other items for ascertaining cost of goods sold are quite straight-forward The auditor proceeds methodically through the following sequence:

Step 1 — Inventory at beginning of year
Step 2 — Purchases (less personal use withdrawals)
Step 3 — Direct labor (manufacturing, mining, etc.)
Step 4 — Materials and supplies (raw)
Step 5 — Other direct costs (freight-in, vendor services, liability insurance, permits and licenses, etc.)
Step 6 — Total costs (ADD 1 through 5)
Step 7 — Inventory at end of year
Step 8 — Cost of Goods Sold (SUBTRACT 7 from 6)

All costs directly associated with attaining and maintaining an inventory are ultimately allowed. That is, they are allowed only after the inventory is sold . . . or abandoned.

New Capitalization Trap

There's no end to the IRS's scheming to lock up money expenditures into inventory. Towards this end, a new capitalization trap was enacted by Congress in late 1986. This trap is called the *uniform capitalization* rule. Statutorily, this rule consists of about 2,500 words in Section 263A: *Capitalization and Inclusion in Inventory Costs of Certain Expenses.* The term "certain expenses" refers to **indirect** costs such as pensions, rent, interest, property taxes, insurance, utilities, repairs, storage, etc. The idea is to allocate to inventory a proportionate share of otherwise deductible operating costs of doing business as a manufacturer or reseller.

Believe it or not, there are some 150,000 words of regulations behind Section 263A. The IRS can — and does — "snow job" an auditee with its inclusion-in-inventory capitalization assertions. Very few IRS auditors truly understand the scope and purpose of the Section 263A regulations. They dodge telling you about the 12 exceptions: Reg. 1.263A-1(b)(1) through 1.263A-1(b)(12). For example, the capitalization of indirect cost rules do **not** apply to small resellers (with gross sales of less than $10,000,000 annually), qualified creative expenditures (by free lance authors, photographers, artists), research and experimental expenditures, certain farming businesses, and "de minimis" indirect costs up to $200,000.

All we can say is that if you get some adamant auditor who wants to snow you with Section 263A, request that he/she cite for you the 12 regulatory exceptions. For most readers of this book, the exceptions will rule out the applicability of Section 263A. But, you don't want to be caught unprepared.

7

INFORMANT REPORTINGS

The Series Of Forms W-2, 1099, and K-1 Is Symptomatic Of "Big Brother Creep" Into Our Tax Lives. Nevertheless, DON'T GO To An Audit Without Searching For, Reviewing, And Matching These Informant Reportings Of Your Income With Corresponding Entries On Your Return. Otherwise, You'll Be In For A Surprise . . . PLUS A 20% Negligence Penalty. Also, Before Audit, PREVIEW Your Allowable Deductions, Expenses, And Credits. Then RECOMPUTE Your Tax. If "Off" By 10% Or More, Prepare An AMENDED RETURN (Form 1040X) And Present It At First Opportunity BEFORE Examination Begins.

We have one basic message that permeates throughout this book. That message is: When going to an IRS audit, **do not go unprepared.** An auditor is not your friend, and has no obligation — other than minor civil courtesies — to guide you through the audit process with the least pain to your pocketbook. An auditor's job is to find some pretense for assessing more tax and thereby collecting more money from you.

One of the most IRS-cherished pretense games has to do with "informant reportings." These are those series of Forms W-2, 1099, and K-1 that we mentioned (only briefly) in Chapters 2 and 5. These are called *information returns*. They provide information to the IRS agent about your lifestyle, your sources of income, and major expenditures such as mortgage interest. The information reported must appear on specific lines and schedules of your tax return. All informants who report their information to the IRS are supposed to provide you with a paper copy of each of their reports. The reports to you may be on official forms or on substitute forms.

Most taxpayers do not take these informant reportings seriously. Many are genuinely puzzled and confused by them. Aware of a taxpayer/auditee's quandary over the proper tax return "matchings," the IRS gloats in its waiting game for entrapping you at time of audit. It has a summary printout of ALL informant reportings made to it, concerning payments to you for the tax year at issue.

In this chapter, therefore, we want to acquaint you with some of the more common oversights that you may have made with respect to certain informant reportings. You need to know how to scan these reportings — and use them — for your own audit protection. Furthermore, you need to have all those informant reportings organized and **at** your fingertips when you go in for the audit. The IRS has a disturbingly high error rate in its summary printouts.

Big Brother Everywhere

The IRS is absolutely ecstatic over the perceived success of its Big Brother informant program. Over the years, it has subtly created a vast network of informants who must report to it . . . or else. Because of the dramatic revenue potential with the use of informants, Congress has gone along with this "big brother creep" of the IRS. As a result, Congress has enacted some *50 separate* informant reporting laws. These laws span the gamut from IR Code Section 6031 (income from partnerships) through Section 6060 (information on income tax preparers).

Don't let the numerical sequencing from Section 6031 through Section 6060 mislead you. Some numerical sections are followed by alphanumeric sections. For example, there are 14 separate reportings required under Section 6050, designated as—

    6050 A — Certain fishing boat operations
    6050 B — Unemployment compensation
    6050 D — Energy grants and financing
    6050 E — State/local income tax refunds
    6050 F — Social security benefits
    6050 G — Railroad retirement benefits

6050 H — Mortgage interest received from individuals
6050 I — Cash received in a trade or business
6050 J — Foreclosures and abandonments of security
6050 K — Exchanges of partnership interests
6050 L — Certain dispositions of donated property
6050 M — Persons receiving Federal contracts
6050 N — Payments of royalties (oil, gas, timber, etc.)
6050 P — Cancellation of certain indebtedness

The most widely known of all 50-some information reportings is Form W-2 (Wage and Tax Statement). Its genesis goes back to 1954 when the first income tax withholding law went into effect. Any tax withholdings by an employer meant that some type of information report to the IRS would have to be made. Furthermore, a separate report would have to be made on each employee.

The first W-2 reporting law was Section 6051: *Receipts for Employees*. Then, it was a simple reporting of gross wages paid and the amount of income tax withheld. Other than the employer's and employee's names, tax IDs, and addresses, there were just two information boxes on the reporting form. Today, there are 21 — yes, **21** — separate information boxes on a W-2. A few boxes contain multiple items of information. For example, Box 13 on Form W-2 accommodates 15 code letters for identifying other information on an employee. This is what we mean by "big brother creep" in our tax system.

And, of course, there has to be some penalty imposed on the informant to make the informant system work. In general, the informant penalty is $50 for "each failure" up to a maximum penalty of $250,000 for large informants. For "small informants" (those whose gross receipts are not more than $5,000,000), the maximum penalty each year is $100,000.

For stiff penalties like these, what informant is going to risk keeping the IRS monkey on his back when he can shift it to yours?

Box 1 on Form W-2

Because Form W-2 is so widely known, it is an excellent primer on the tactics that the IRS uses with regard to all informant reportings. The premier tactic of the IRS is what we call *maximum gross* reporting. By this tactic, the IRS forces the informant to report the maximum possible taxable amount without any deductions, exemptions, or credits whatsoever. The IRS also forces into the gross amount various nontaxable items, expense reimbursements, noncash benefits, prizes and awards, and other items. When we tell you what the IRS mandates that your employer include in Box 1, you will understand better what the maximum gross tactic is.

Of the 21 boxes of information on Form W-2, Box 1 is really the only one in which the IRS is interested. This box is officially captioned—

Wages, tips, other compensation

Have you any idea how extensive and inclusive this caption is?

Here's what the instructions to your employer say when he enters an amount in Box 1 on Form W-2:

Show in Box 1, before any payroll deductions, the following items:
1. *Total wages (excluding elective deferrals), prizes, and awards paid to employees during the year.*
2. *Total noncash payments (including certain fringe benefits).*
3. *Total tips reported by employee to employer.*
4. *Certain employee business expense reimbursements.*
5. *The cost of (certain) accident and health insurance premiums.*
6. *Taxable benefits made from a section 125 (cafeteria) plan.*
7. *Group-term life insurance in excess of $50,000.*
8. *The amount paid for educational assistance that is not job related.*
9. *The amount of your employees share of taxes paid by you.*
10. *All other compensation (such as) bonuses, commissions, vacation allowances, sick pay, scholarships, grants, taxable payments for moving expenses, and other payments from which Federal income tax is not withheld.*

Your "Copy C" of Form W-2 has instructions which say—

Enter this amount [from Box 1] *on the wages line of your tax return. If you are required to file a tax return, a negligence penalty or other sanction may be imposed on you if this income is taxable and you fail to report it.*

The wages line on your tax return is captioned—

Wages, salaries, tips, etc. Attach Form(s) W-2

Now, you have the key idea behind all informant reportings: not just the W-2s. The idea is to force the informant to report to the IRS the maximum possible tax accountable amount while simultaneously threatening you with a negligence penalty for not exact-matching that amount on your own return. Pursuant to Section 6662(a), the negligence penalty is 20%. Consequently, when going to an audit, you want all information returns of the same type grouped together, and the "Box 1s" thereto totaled.

Form 1098: Mortgage Interest

Another IRS tactic behind the informant reportings is to key each class of information return to a distinct separate line on your tax return. By having distinctly separate lines for each information class (remember, there are about 50 such classes), the IRS's Big Computer can do its own cross-checking and matching that which you report. This way, if you fail to report, or underreport, or misreport on a different line, the IRS has you up against its stone wall. This is what we call the *distinctive line* tactic. It is a "tactic" in that you can be caught unprepared at time of audit if you don't know about it.

The best example of distinctive line matching is Form 1098: Mortgage Interest Statement. This form has four information boxes, the key one being Box 1 (of course). This Box 1 is captioned—

Mortgage interest received from payer(s)/borrower(s)*

Be sure to note the asterisk (*). The asterisk refers to a headnote on Form 1098 (Copy B) which says—

> *The amount shown may not be fully deductible by you on your tax return. Limitations . . . may apply. In addition, you may only deduct an amount of mortgage interest to the extent it was incurred by you, actually paid by you, and not reimbursed by another person.*

In other words, when you have a potential deduction amount being informant reported, you are IRS cautioned about its applicable limitations. The limitations depend on the proper line **and** the proper schedule where you claim the deduction.

The amount in Box 1 of a Form 1098 must go on one of the following captioned lines on one of the following applicable schedules, namely:

Schedule A: Itemized Deductions
— *Home mortgage interest reported on Form 1098*

Schedule C: Profit or Loss from Business
— *Mortgage interest paid to banks, etc.*

Schedule E: Supplemental Income and Loss
— *Mortgage interest paid to banks, etc.*

Schedule F: Profit or Loss from Farming
— *Mortgage interest paid to banks, etc.*

If you have a mortgage with more than one financial institution, you'll receive a Form 1098 from each. This means that you have to match each 1098 with each kind of property (Schedule A, C, E, or F) being mortgaged. If you have multiple mortgages with the same company, you have to allocate the Box 1 amount among each applicable schedule. Distinct line entry and schedule matching is a challenge of its own.

If you overreport one distinctive line and underreport on another, the auditor will disallow the amount overreported, and will accept the amount underreported. For example, suppose the proper amounts to be reported (deducted) on Schedules A and E were $9,000 and $6,000 respectively. You claimed $10,000 on Schedule A (which is $1,000 overclaimed) and $5,000 on Schedule E (which is $1,000 underclaimed). You lose $2,000 of deductible mortgage interest simply because you didn't enter the correct amounts on the right lines and schedules. The IRS is viciously line-entry conscious, which is why its 50-some informant laws are so revenue successful. You miss the proper entry line, you miss the tax benefit.

Schedule K-1 (1065): Partnerships

There is one informant return that causes more loss of tax benefits than any other single type. This is Schedule K-1 (1065): Partner's Share of Income, Credits, Deductions, Etc. A K-1 (Form 1065) consists of about 50 boxes of tax information. Yes — 50! The first 12 boxes consist of income and loss information. The other 38 boxes consist of credits and deductions which pass through from the partnership to each partner.

Of the 12 income lines, 9 may be negative amounts (meaning losses) as well as being positive amounts. Guess what happens to any negative (loss) income entries on Schedule K-1?

The IRS's computer NEVER PICKS UP YOUR NEGATIVE INCOME AMOUNTS. It picks up only your positives! This is the tactic we call: *seeing positives only.*

For example, you could have on a K-1 one positive income entry showing $5,000 and six negative income entries totaling <$23,000>. Technically, if all partnership income were of the same tax character (which it is not), you would have a net income loss of <$18,000> [23,000 − 5,000]. Also, technically, if the IRS were not so dishonest in its computer matching programming, the <$18,000> income loss would be used to offset whatever positive income you have on other informant returns. But, this does **not** happen. The IRS computer picks up only the $5,000 positive income on your K-1, and adds it to all other positives-only income amounts on other informant reports to it.

You are left entirely on your own to claim the negative income amounts (and your credits and deductions) on the proper lines on other forms and schedules that attach to your return. Similar tactics apply to Schedules K-1 (1041): Estates and Trusts, and K-1 (1120): S corporations.

Form 1099-S: Realty Sales

Undoubtedly, the most reckless of all IRS-mandated informant returns is Form 1099-S. This form is titled: Proceeds from Real Estate Transactions. It contains five information boxes. The key box that the IRS is interested in is Box 2: *Gross Proceeds*. This is the full gross selling price of the real property involved. The IRS computer treats the gross sale price as another source of W-2 income, if the amount is not precisely reported on your tax return.

Most real estate transactions involve gross dollar amounts ranging from $100,000 to $1,000,000 or more. These are awfully big numbers to be whirling around in the IRS's computer, waiting to snag you. The instructions on Form 1099-S warn you of negligence and other penalties that can be imposed if you fail to report the full amount . . . whether taxable or not. This is a tactic we call: *lacking proper instructions*.

In Chapter 6, we explained the role of cost or other basis in an asset that someday might be sold. Whatever your tax basis is in a parcel of real estate sold comes back to you as "return of capital." It is not taxed. But there is no box on Form 1099-S for entering this information for the IRS to see. Instead you have to fish around on your own, and enter your basis information on such forms as—

Form 2119: Sale of Your Home
Form 4797: Sales of Business Property
Form 6252: Installment Sale Income
Schedule D (Form 1040): Capital Gains and Losses

Most real property is owned by two or more persons: rarely by one person alone. When there are co-owners, only one person's name (and Tax ID) appears on Form 1099-S. This name is usually that person whose name appears first on the title to the property being transferred. For example, if there were three co-owners: A at 20%, B at 30%, and C at 50%, A's name only would appear. Yet, technically, each co-owner is tax responsible only for his/her ownership percentage of the property. So, why is one person dunned for the whole gross proceeds amount?

The simple answer is: the IRS doesn't care. It is up to the co-owners themselves to instruct the escrow officer closing the real estate transaction to issue *multiple* 1099-Ss. The total gross proceeds could then be apportioned according to each co-owner's ownership percentage (as depicted in Figure 7.1). If the IRS were a conscientious and caring agency, it would provide a headnote instruction to this effect directly on Form 1099-S.

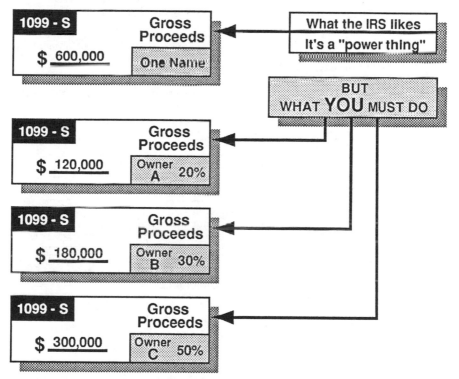

Fig. 7.1 - Proportionate Separate Forms 1099-S for Multiple Co-Owners

Menu of Form 1099s

We've barely touched on the information reporting problems of only one Form 1099: the 11th. There are 10 other such forms. We list all 11 for you in Figure 7.2. Please take a moment and scan down this list.

Form	Title	Information Reported
1099 - A	Acquisition or abandonment of secured property	Description and value of property on which debt was owed, and abandoned (or acquired by another).
1099 - B	Proceeds From Broker Transactions and Barter Exchanges	Sales or redemptions of securities, commodities, futures transactions, and barter transactions.
1099 - C	Cancellation of Debt	Cancellation of debt owed to a financial institution, credit union, or government agency.
1099 - DIV	Dividends and Distributions	Dividends, capital gain distributions, nontaxable distributions, and distributions in liquidation.
1099 - G	Certain Government Payments	Unemployment compensation, state/local income tax refunds, agricultural payments, and taxable grants.
1099 - INT	Interest Income	Interest income derived from all interest-bearing accounts, except IRAs.
1099 - MISC	Miscellaneous Income	See text and Fig. 7.3.
1099 - OID	Original Issue Discount	Difference between stated redemption price at maturity, and issue price of a bond, note, or debt.
1099 - PATR	Taxable Distributions From (Farm) Cooperatives	Patronage dividends paid in cash, written notices of allocation, or other property.
1099 - R	Distributions From Retirement Plans, IRAs, Insurance Contracts, Etc.	Distributions from pensions, annuities, profit-sharing plans, IRAs, SEPs, or Insurance Contracts.
1099 - S	Proceeds From Real Estate Transactions	Gross proceeds from the sale or exchange of real estate: residential, nonresidential, farmland, etc.

Fig. 7.2 - List of Variant Forms of 1099 "Information Returns"

As to some of the 1099s in Figure 7.2, you may not have heard of them before. Yet, somewhere in all of your "tax papers and things" one or more of those forms may be buried. You may not know if one of those odd ones is there. Even if there, you may not recognize it. It doesn't shout at you. Yet, when you go in for audit, you can be sure that every Form 1099 issued in your name and Tax ID will be known to the auditor. This is the marvel of our electronic information age.

Of the entire Form 1099 series, the most commonly known ones are:

1099-INT	: Interest Income
1099-DIV	: Dividends and Distributions
1099-B	: Proceeds from Broker Transactions
1099-G	: Certain Government Payments
1099-R	: Distribution from Retirement Plans, IRAs, etc.

These "five trojans" are reported to the IRS when payments to you are as made for as low as $10. We've actually seen these 1099s issued for as low as *10 cents*! When will all of this electronic surveillance of our financial affairs ever stop?

What Figure 7.2 does not show is that there is also an informant surveillance form designated as W-2G. The "G" is for *Gambling Winnings*. That is, if you derive winnings — NOT losses — from horse racing, dog racing, jai alai, lotteries, sweepstakes, or wagering pools of $600 or more, you are informed on to the IRS. If you win $1,200 or more from bingo or slot machines, Form W-2G is used. If you win $1,500 or more from keno, another W-2G is prepared. It's a pretty tight web that Big Brother is weaving.

A 1099 for "Each Account"

What is not further revealed in Figure 7.2 is that a *separate* Form 1099 is required on each financial transaction that you incur. It is not uncommon for a financially active taxpayer to receive 15, 30, even 50 or more 1099s for a given tax year.

If you own, say, five accounts with separate banking, brokerage, or financial institutions (including mutual funds and insurance companies), you'll receive a separate Form 1099 from each account custodian. But, chances are, the five different 1099s will not be readily identifiable. Each 1099 informant is permitted to use its own letterhead and format to transmit to you on paper the same information that it transmits electronically to the IRS. Because all Figure 7-2 Forms 1099 do not look alike, overlooking them and mistaking them is commonplace. This means that you have to read every piece of paper coming to you from your account informant. You need to do this to identify those which are "tax information" with a small-printed "1099" thereon.

If you are an active brokerage firm or mutual fund trader, you have a severe tax return matching problem on your hands. Every transaction (sale, redemption, exchange, contract expiration) that you make is a SEPARATE REPORTABLE EVENT. If you make 50 transactions for the year, for example, your own tax return must show each and every one of those 50 transactions.

Keep in mind that for every transaction event, the *gross proceeds only* are electronically transmitted to the IRS. The total gross proceeds for the year from all of your transaction events is what the IRS sees in your name and Tax ID. If, for example, you churn a $10,000 securities account 20 times during the year, the total gross proceeds that the IRS would see would be $200,000 (20 x $10,000). You could have an overall net loss for the year of <$5,000>. Yet, the IRS wants to tax you on the $200,000.

To prove your <$5,000> net loss, you have to enter each of your 20 transactions separately on your return, listing your "cost or other basis" for each respective transaction. Separately, you compute the gain or loss for each transaction. Then you show a net gain or loss for the year. This is where your Schedule D (Form 1040): Capital Gains and Losses, gets a workout.

Our experience has been that, when there are more than 10 separate transactions listed on Schedule D, an IRS auditor will randomly select three transactions for "testing" you. If your substantiation checks out on the sample selections, the auditor will then compare the total gross proceeds on your Schedule D with the total that he/she has on the printouts from your informants. If the match is within 2% or 3% — called "de minimis variance" — your accounting will be accepted. If the mismatch is more than 5%, you have some serious explaining or more homework to do.

Form 1099-MISC: The Catchall

If you will note in Figure 7.2, we omitted any description of what is reported on Form 1099-MISC: *Miscellaneous Income.* A short description is that it includes everything else that is not specifically reported on the 10 other Forms 1099 and Form W-2G. The IRS description of what is reported on 1099-MISC is—

Rent or royalty payments; prizes and awards that are not for services, such as winnings on TV or radio shows.

Payments to crew members by owners or operators of fishing boats [and] *payments of proceeds from sale of catch.*

Payments to a physician, physician's corporation, or other supplier of health and medical services . . . by medical assistance programs or health and accident insurance plans.

Payments for services performed for a trade or business by persons not treated as employees, [such as] *fees to subcontractor or consultants, expenses* [reimbursed] *to a nonemployee, and golden parachute payments.*

Substitute dividend and tax-exempt interest payments reportable by brokers. Crop insurance proceeds.

The reporting thresholds on Form 1099-MISC are: (a) $1 or more for payments to crew members of fishing boats, (b) $10 or more for royalties and substitute dividends, (c) $600 or more for all except direct sales persons, and (d) $5,000 or more of consumer products to a buyer for direct resale.

A condensed arrangement of the dollar information boxes on Form 1099-MISC is presented in Figure 7.3. When you glance at the number of reporting options available to payer informants, you can appreciate why this one form is the most misused and abused information return of all (including some we haven't yet told you about). If a payer pays you money for whatever reason, and wants to claim a tax deduction for it, he reports it on Form 1099-MISC

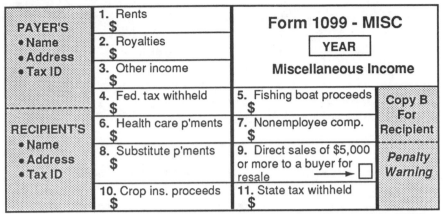

PAYER'S • Name • Address • Tax ID	1. Rents $	Form 1099 - MISC	
	2. Royalties $	YEAR	
	3. Other income $	Miscellaneous Income	
	4. Fed. tax withheld $	5. Fishing boat proceeds $	Copy B For Recipient
RECIPIENT'S • Name • Address • Tax ID	6. Health care p'ments $	7. Nonemployee comp. $	
	8. Substitute p'ments $	9. Direct sales of $5,000 or more to a buyer for ☐ resale →	Penalty Warning
	10. Crop ins. proceeds $	11. State tax withheld $	

Fig. 7.3 - Enlargement of the "Information Boxes" on Form 1099 - MISC

whether he is required to or not. This leaves you holding the bag for accounting to the IRS for money that may not be taxable.

To illustrate the abusive use of Form 1099-MISC by some payers, we tell you of a recent true case. It was a divorce situation. The husband, an attorney, agreed to pay his ex-wife $3,000,000 as a property settlement. This is "division of property money." It is not taxable when received by the ex-wife. It is not tax deductible when paid by the ex-husband. Yet, the attorney ex-husband set up a business trust for his children and grandchildren from which he dispersed $150,000 each year to this ex-wife. He reported the payments in Box 7 of Form 1099-MISC as *Nonemployee compensation*. He, of course, took a business expense deduction for it. The ex-wife had to report the amount as income on Schedule C (Form 1040): Profit or Loss from Business. She then had to negate out the entire $150,000 amount on the line captioned: *Other expenses*. She added an explanation that the amount was for partial payment of a property settlement under a Decree of Divorce.

Each year, the ex-wife attaches a separate statement to her return, citing the property settlement terms and Section 1041(a) of the IR Code re nontaxable transfers of property between spouses incident to divorce. Each year, also, she requests that the IRS instruct the payer (ex-husband attorney) to desist from filing abusive 1099-MISCs. But, each year, the IRS refuses to take any corrective action. Consequently, each year the ex-wife has to go through the same *negating out* routine, in order to avoid being taxed on informant money that is statutorily nontaxable.

The above true case highlights a glaring fault in the IRS informant reporting program. In its ecstasy over its great success, the IRS does nothing about abuses by disreputable informants.

Other Surveillance Reports

Form 1099-MISC is not the end of the information reporting program. There are other miscellaneously numbered forms, via which the IRS is electronically informed of various financial activities. As of this writing, there are at least 10 others not previously mentioned. We'll cite just a few examples to add spice and flavor to the above.

You see an ad in the used car columns of your local newspaper — or on the Internet — listing a late model luxury auto for $15,000. You confirm its bluebook value, then call the phone number given. You like what you hear, and start dickering with the seller over the price. He sounds a little annoyed, then says—

"Look, this is a $15,000 bluebook valued vehicle. You've probably already checked this out yourself. I'll tell you what. You give me $11,000 cash — cold, green paper cash — and I'll let you have it. That's a saving to you of $4,000."

You respond: "O.K. Sounds great! I'll get the cash for you."

You go to your local bank, or credit union, or wherever your savings are, and draw out $11,000 in cash. The teller looks at you quizzically, asking for some identification, your social security number, and your birth date. Thinking nothing of it, you give whatever information the teller asks for. You get the cash in hand and walk out. Before the close of day, the teller fills out **Form 4789**: Currency Transaction Report, and mails it off to the IRS. A few months later, you get a certified mail computer demand from the IRS wanting to know why the $11,000 cash and what you did with the money. There are threats of penalties, inferring that you are involved in drug dealing and/or money laundering.

If you sold your own car for $11,000 cash and took the green paper to deposit it in your saving bank, the teller there would ask identifying questions similar to the above. In addition, you would be asked to give your occupation, business, or profession, and to identify the type of transaction from which you derived the $11,000. The teller then completes **Form 8300**: Report of Cash Payment over $10,000, and sends it on the IRS.

You attend a high-pressure investment seminar which whips you into a frenzy about the great tax benefits of using foreign trusts, foreign corporations, and foreign partnerships. Along with others, you put up $10,000 to participate in the foreign entity. You do so, little realizing that the promoter, or the transferor of funds, has to prepare and submit to the IRS one or more such forms as **926, 5471, 5472, 8308, 8362** . . . and possibly others. These are variant reports of foreign financial transactions which the IRS likes to keep under surveillance continually.

Lining Things Up

Winning an audit is somewhat like playing a poker game. The key difference is that there is no 5-card limit per hand, and the only bluffing that takes place is by the IRS. Consequently, your only trumping opportunity is to be so well prepared that you can call the IRS's bluff before the auditor gets you cornered. This means lining up your ducks — all of those informant reports and your proof documents — well ahead of time. The organizational effort for doing this is summarized in Figure 7.4.

Your first opportunity to out-bluff the IRS is when, after introductory courtesies and preliminary questioning, the auditor says (to the effect)—

"Before we start the examination, is there anything that you would like to tell me about your return that is not on your return? Anything at all?"

The inference is that the IRS *may* be holding some information against you that is not on your return. This is an **inference** only.

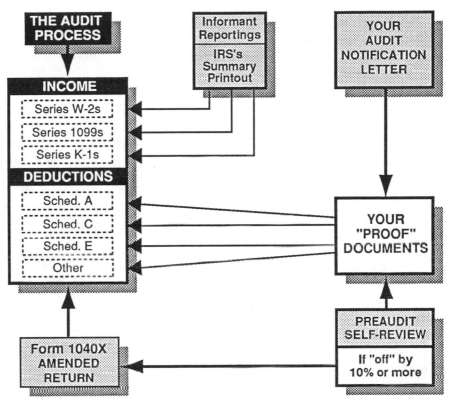

Fig. 7.4 - Organizational Effort Required for Good Audit Preparation

Don't let it disorient you into a religious confessional of every tax sin in your distant past. Instead, seize the opportunity.

If, after a diligent review of all informant reports for which you have copies (the W-2s, 1099s, and K-1s), there is some underreporting or misreporting of income, get those cards on the table immediately. Point out to the auditor, step by step, every *significant* inconsistency that you have uncovered on your own. Doing so will free your mind and put you more on the offensive than defensive. By "significant," we mean only those inconsistencies which are more than 5% variance from the items on your return. Keeping the minor inconsistencies to yourself gives you a psychological edge (of knowing there's likely to be no big surprise) when the examination proceeds.

After clearing away the significant income-type inconsistencies (if any), your next cards-on-the-table effort is to focus on underclaimed (or overclaimed) personal deductions, business expenses, and allowable credits. Not every taxpayer aggressively claims every deduction-type dollar to which he may be entitled. But once you are subject to the hassle of an audit, claim every overlooked deduction dollar that you possibly can. Or, if you have overclaimed, admit to it. Do it up front. Don't wait until the auditor brings up the item later in the examination. Otherwise, the auditor will say (in effect)—

"I gave you the opportunity earlier, but you didn't take advantage of it. It's too late now. Sorry."

If your income and deduction inconsistencies amount to a tax variance of 10% or more of the tax shown on your original return, prepare an *Amended Return*: **Form 1040X**. Show on it all corrections that you want considered. If your recomputations show an additional tax to pay, have a payment check written out and attached to the 1040X. Then, plop it down in front of the auditor and say—

"This is my amended return for _____(year)_____ showing the items that I've just brought to your attention. Please have your audit notes show that this 1040X was presented to you **before** your examination began."

Yes, this will tee off the auditor a bit. This is because you will have taken some of the mystique and wind out of his/her audit sails. But don't worry. You are getting your message across. That message is: You are prepared; you are loaded for bear; you want to get going on the examination specifics.

8

SCHEDULE A ITEMS

There Are Approximately 25 Line-Entry Deductions On Schedule A (Form 1040). Several Are Affected By Specific AGI (Adjusted Gross Income) Amounts. Others Are Limited By Statutory Wording, And By the Attachment of Separate Computational Forms. The Largest Single Deduction, Home Mortgage Interest, Can Become A "Computer Matching" Nightmare. Disaster Losses Have A "Carryback" Feature Whereas Large Contributions Have A "Carryforward" Feature. Be Sure To Enter The Correct Deduction On The Correct Official Line Number.

Schedule A (Form 1040) is officially titled: **Itemized Deductions**. This is too general, as there are other schedules and forms on which deductions also are itemized. More properly, the Schedule A heading should be: Itemized **Personal** Deductions. This is because those deductions on Schedule A are more personalized in nature than pure business-type deductions.

Schedule A is the very first attachment to Form 1040: U.S. Individual Income Tax Return. It is the most commonly used schedule of all attachments to Form 1040. Nearly half of all individual tax returns include Schedule A. This means that about 50,000,000 (50 million) Schedule A's go through the system each year. It is for this reason that Schedule A is one of the prime targets for audit. It has a lot of deduction items on it, at least one or two of which every auditor wants to knock out.

There are approximately 25 separate deduction entries on Schedule A. A number of these entries are backed up with supporting forms of their own. The most prominent ones are:

Form 1098 — Home Mortgage Interest
Form 2106 — Employee Business Expenses
Form 4684 — Casualties and Thefts
Form 4952 — Investment Interest Expense
Form 8283 — Noncash Charitable Contributions
Other Miscellaneous Deductions (from list)

Because of the vast number of potential entries and supporting entries associated with Schedule A, it is rare indeed that an auditor would attempt to examine each line sequentially. Instead, an auditor will pick and choose those items with which he/she is most familiar, and for which his/her own experience has proven lucrative for performance quota banking. This means that an experienced auditor will pick the "tricky points" on which to nail you.

Consequently, in this chapter we'll address the tricky points on Schedule A, rather than engaging in a line-by-line analysis of all possible entries on the form.

Specific AGI Thresholds

In its drive to curtail the benefits of Schedule A, Congress has imposed certain thresholds that must be dollar exceeded, before certain entries can be made. There are at least four of these thresholds. All are referenced to **AGI**: *Adjusted Gross Income.*

Gross income, as its name implies, is the total income from all sources enumerated in Section 61 (which we discussed in Chapter 5). Rarely will an auditor attack Schedule A, until he has at least perused your total income. Against total income, certain adjustments are — or may be — made. There are some six to eight adjustments authorized by Section 62: Adjusted Gross Income. For example, alimony paid is a subtraction from (adjustment to) one's total income. But, generally speaking, most Form 1040 filers have no adjustments; some have one adjustment; a few have two; and rarely are there three or more. So these adjustments are not important to our discussion at this point.

Nevertheless, each taxpayer's own AGI is an important reference before entering Schedule A. Certain items in Schedule A are curtailed by a specific percentage of one's AGI. The particular AGI-limited items are:

1. Miscellaneous expenses : 2 % AGI
2. Medical expenses   : 7.5% AGI
3. Casualties and thefts   : 10 % AGI
4. Charitable contributions : 50 % AGI

Now you see why an auditor, before attacking your Schedule A, will first satisfy himself as to his version of your correct AGI. The higher he can force your AGI, the less work he has to do on Schedule A. Some entries would automatically go away, based on dollar comparisons alone.

So important is this point that we present in Figure 8.1 example dollar thresholds that must be exceeded before each of three of the four items above can be entered. Note that we have selected four "typical" AGIs, namely: $35,000; $50,000; $85,000; and $150,000. This is probably the range in which the much maligned "middle income taxpayer" is hounded for more taxes.

At any rate, the message in Figure 8.1 is that the higher your AGI, the less likely that certain entries will appear in Schedule A. We'll expand on these AGI-sensitive items below.

ADJUSTED GROSS INCOME	NOT DEDUCTIBLE BELOW THESE AMOUNTS		
"Middle-Income" Taxpayer	2% AGI Miscellaneous Deductions	7.5% AGI Medical Expenses	10% AGI Casualty Losses
$35,000	700	2,625	3,500
$50,000	1,000	3,750	5,000
$85,000	1,700	6,375	8,500
$150,000	3,000	11,250	15,000

Fig. 8.1 - Specific AGI Thresholds Before Entering Schedule A

Miscellaneous Expenses: 2% AGI

The term "miscellaneous expenses" covers a whole host of odds and ends that, technically, are allowable, but are small in dollar amount per item. For example, most every middle-income taxpayer incurs some occupationally-related expenditures such as union dues, professional fees, tools, supplies, and the like. Those who have their returns prepared professionally also pay tax preparation fees. Taken together, seldom do all of these expenditures exceed $1,000. Except for the lower AGIs, the *2% floor* (as it is called) pretty well rules these items out as a Schedule A miscellaneous entry.

The 2% floor came about at the prodding of Congress by the IRS. The IRS wanted to reduce its workload and make it easier on itself to drag in more taxpayer money to please Congress. So, in 1986, Congress enacted Section 67: *2-percent Foor on Miscellaneous Itemized Deductions.* Section 67(a) sets forth the general rule as—

In the case of an individual, the miscellaneous itemized deductions for any taxable year shall be allowed only to the extent that the aggregate of such deductions exceeds 2 percent of adjusted gross income.

There are a few statutory exemptions to the 2% floor . . . but not many. The purpose of Section 67 was to sweep in all such expenditures as employee unreimbursed expenses, tuition, books, investment expenses, safe-deposit boxes, tools, uniforms, supplies, educational courses, teaching aids, appraisal fees, legal fees (for collecting income), and personalized on-the-job equipment such as lap-type computers, cellular phones, and family autos.

To make Section 67 more forbidding, the IRS promulgated tons of regulations — some 16,000 words — to prevent the 2% floor from being bypassed. The rule now applies to partnerships, S corporations, grantor trusts, decedent estates, and nonpublicly offered regulated investment companies.

Congress was so pleased with IRS's creativity for increasing revenue without increasing tax rates, that it entertained IRS's proposal that only 50% of business meals and entertainment be allowed. Thereupon, Congress enacted Section 274(n), now known as the *50% M & E rule.* Cleverly, the 50% M & E (meals and entertainment) is also folded-in under the 2% floor!

Medical Expenses: 7.5% AGI

Medical expenses have always been one item on Schedule A which has annoyed the IRS. Over the years, the IRS has tried to regulate this one deduction completely out of existence. The reason for IRS's annoyance is that taxpayers are generally well prepared on this one item. An auditor can spend an hour or two picking away at medical documents, only to produce $100 or $200 in disallowances.

Most taxpayers understand the concept of medical expenses, and the need for doctors, dentists, nurses, hospitals, and medication. They dislike incurring these expenses, but once they become sick, injured, or diseased, they want the deduction. They resent the IRS's chameleon behavior: if it can't win a point by the established rules, it tries to change the rules to suit its own ends.

After many years of full medical expense deductions, the IRS induced Congress to set a 2.5% AGI threshold. A few years later, it upped the threshold to 5% AGI. In 1986, it upped the threshold again to 7.5% AGI. Apparently, effort was made to go beyond 7.5% AGI, but Congress finally balked.

Section 213(a): *Medical, Dental, etc. Expenses* casts the 7.5% AGI in concrete as follows:

> *There shall be allowed as a deduction the expenses paid during the taxable year, not compensated for by insurance or otherwise, for medical care of the taxpayer, his spouse, or a dependent . . . to the extent that such expenses exceed 7. 5 percent of adjusted gross income.*

In addition to Section 213(a), special rules were enacted with respect to—

1. Medicines, drugs, and insulin
   — must be prescribed by a physician
2. Medical expenses paid after death
   — up to 1 year
3. Lodging away from home primarily for and essential to medical care
   — up to $50 per night
4. Children of divorced parents
   — whichever parent pays the bill may claim

In its official instructions to Schedule A, the IRS has grouped all medical expenses into two categories: deductible and nondeductible. Examples in each of these categories are:

Deductible medical expenses
— amounts paid for doctors, dentists, nurses, hospitals, prescription medicines, legal drugs, insulin, transportation, lodging, hearing aids, dentures, eyeglasses, contact lenses, wheelchairs, ambulances, other medical aids, and insurance premiums therewith.

Nondeductible medical expenses
— amounts paid for cosmetic surgery (unless for restoration of deformities caused by accident, disease, injury, or trauma), life insurance, medicare tax, nursing care for a healthy baby, hygienic and dietary aids, and doctor-ordered travel for rest or change of environment.

At Line 1 of Schedule A, you are expressly told:

*Enter the **total** of your medical and dental expenses, **after** you reduce the expenses by any payments received from insurance or other sources.* [Emphasis added.]

In other words, substantiation of your insurance reimbursement or other assistance payments, if any, will be sought.

The official instructions also tell you that if you receive any reimbursement or payments in a year subsequent to your entries on Schedule A, you do not reduce the nonapplicable year expenses. Instead, you report any reimbursement for prior-year expenses claimed as "other income" on page 1 (Gross income) of Form 1040.

Casualties and Thefts: 10% AGI

The most difficult item to ever prove on Schedule A is a casualty or theft loss. The rules for deductibility of such losses have been difficult and tricky for years. Such losses first became allowable in 1954.

To get a casualty loss, you first have to prove that there indeed was a casualty (or theft). This is not always tax self-evident. Next, you have to prove your "cost or other basis" (Chapter 6 revisited). Then you must put in a claim for any insurance or other reimbursement, as applicable and appropriate. If the reimbursement is greater than your cost basis, you have a casualty **gain**: not a loss!

Let us illustrate.

Suppose some years ago you bought a parcel of land in the mountains and built a vacation cabin thereon. You paid $6,000 for the land and $20,000 for the cabin structure and built-ins. You kept your insurance up to date and paid increased premiums as the property value increased. On your latest bill, the property was valued at $100,000.

A forest fire gets started in the vicinity of your cabin. It soon rages out of control. When it is all over, your cabin is burned to the ground.

After the usual insurance delays, the company pays you $75,000. Do you have a loss or a gain?

Answer: You have a gain. You have additional tax to pay. Yes, you do!

Just before the fire, your property was worth $100,000. Of this amount, the insurance company figured your land was worth $25,000 (because of its before-fire location, view, and access). So they paid you $75,000 for the cabin structure and built-ins. Though the structure burned to the ground, the land itself did not burn.

Your gain is $55,000. This derives from the $75,000 reimbursement minus your $20,000 cost of the structure. You still have the land. So, you get no Schedule A deduction. But let's go on; there are more gimmicks.

If you had no insurance, you would have an actual loss (on the cabin fire above). Whether it's a tax loss or not is another matter.

Your next step is to establish the *loss in value*: immediately before the casualty and immediately after it. In the illustration above, the loss in value (of the cabin) is clearly $75,000. At this juncture, the tax rules say you must choose **the smaller of** (a) cost or other basis, or (b) loss in value. Your cost of $20,000 is indeed smaller than the $75,000 loss in value. So, it now appears that you have a $20,000 tax loss. Right?

Now the AGI gimmick.

Subsection 165(h)(2)(A) of the tax code says, in part—

*If the personal casualty losses for any taxable year exceed the personal casualty gains for such taxable year, such losses shall be allowed for the taxable year **only to the extent** . . . of such excess as exceeds 10 percent of the adjusted gross income of the individual.* [Emphasis added.]

In other words, there's no Schedule A casualty loss until the "smaller of" the loss exceeds 10% of your AGI. The IRS wins, in part, on this one.

For example, suppose your AGI is $50,000 for the year in which you suffered the $20,000 cabin fire loss. Your 10% AGI is $5,000. Now your Schedule A loss is reduced to a mere $15,000 ($20,000 less $5,000). In reality, your loss in value was $75,000. This means that you have a $60,000 "loss-loss." Personal loss-losses are not tax recognized.

Because casualty loss computations are rather complicated, we present in Figure 8.2 the sequential steps for computing such a loss. The instructions on Schedule A tell you to: *Attach Form 4684* (Casualties and Thefts). The presentation in Figure 8.2 is an edited abridgment of Form 4684.

Charitable Contributions: 50% AGI

There's just one more AGI feature on Schedule A that we should comment on. This is the 50% AGI limitation for contributions and gifts to charity. Other than its large 50% figure, this limitation differs in one distinctive respect from the other AGI's above. It has a *carryover* feature. We'll explain.

Gifts to bona fide charitable organizations or public entities with charitable, religious, educational, fraternal, or prevention of cruelty purposes have been deductible items of long standing. For taxpayers with strong donative bent, it is possible to virtually eliminate all tax with this one deduction alone. This is where the 50% AGI limitation comes in.

The tax code addresses all charitable contributions and gifts in Section 170. Subsection 170(b)(1)(A) thereunder states, in part—

In the case of an individual, the deduction . . . shall be allowed to the extent that the aggregate of such contributions does not exceed 50 percent of the taxpayer's contribution base for the taxable year.

This is quite clear and self-explanatory. But when we look at Schedule A, different words appear.

The "gifts to charity" portion of Schedule A is arranged into three specific line entries. These three lines are:

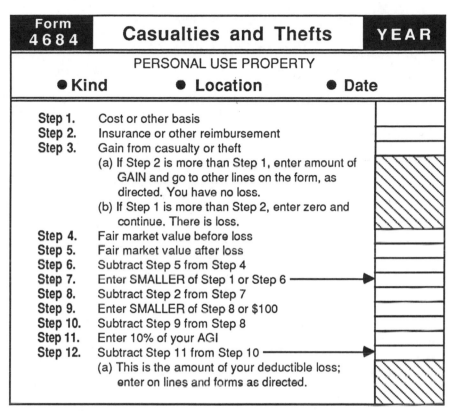

Fig. 8.2 - Steps (Form 4684) For Casualty Loss Deduction

1. Gifts by cash or check
2. Other than by cash or check
3. Carryover from prior year

Instructions on Schedule A at entries 1 and 2 say—

If you made any one gift of $250 or more, see [separate instructions]. *You may deduct* [such] *gift only if you have a statement from the charitable organization showing: (1) The amount of any money contributed and a description of any property donated, and (2) Whether the organization did or did not give you any goods or services in return for your contribution.*

In addition, instructions to the second entry say—

*If over $500, you **MUST** attach Form 8283.*

There are no instructions (on Schedule A) with regard to the third line: Carryover from prior year.

Form 8283: Noncash Charitable Contributions, is very formidable. It is organized into six parts as follows:

Section A   — Items aggregating $5,000 or less
• Part I   — Information on donated property
• Part II   — Donative intent and restrictions, if any

Section B   — Items aggregating more than $5,000
• Part I   — Information on donated property
• Part II   — Taxpayer (donor) statement
• Part III   — Certification of appraiser
• Part IV   — Donee acknowledgment

In other words, if over $500 noncash is contributed, much detailed information must be submitted with one's return.

If the total of cash (Line 1) and noncash (Line 2) exceeds 50% AGI, subsection 170(d)(1)(A) comes into play. The essence of this subsection is that—

In the case of an individual, if the amount of charitable contribution . . . within a taxable year . . . exceeds 50 percent of the taxpayer's contribution base for such year, such excess shall be treated as a charitable contribution . . . paid in each of the 5 succeeding taxable years in order of time.

In other words, the excess can be "carried over" to one or more subsequent years.

This is where Line 3 above (Carryover from prior year) comes in. This carryover of an amount in excess of the AGI limitation does not appear anyplace else on Schedule A. If you make an entry on this carryover line, you can be sure that it will be audit examined. This could open up your prior-year **and** your subsequent-year tax returns also.

Deductible Taxes: No AGI

There are a number of entry lines on Schedule A which are not subject to AGI limitations of any kind. But they have their own peculiarities. It is the peculiarities — not the well known — that auditors focus on. Deductible taxes is a case in point.

Most taxpayers feel, and rightly so, that all taxes of any kind should be fully deductible on Form 1040. Governments are so clever in how they designate mandatory revenue collections. They avoid the T-word ("T" for taxes) like a plague. All mandatory contributions to government entities should be fully deductible, the same way that charitable contributions are. But this is not the case.

Only three types of taxes can be entered on Schedule A. These are—

- State/local income taxes
- Real estate taxes
- Personal property taxes

Excluded are social security taxes, sales taxes, gasoline taxes, telephone taxes, custom duties, gift taxes, death taxes, improvement taxes, license fees, and so on.

State and local income taxes are deductible only in the year actually paid. This includes foreign income taxes and "state disability insurance" which *is* a tax on income. If any income taxes are in arrears, you get the deduction (exclusive of penalties and interest) when you pay them. You know, of course, that you cannot deduct your prior year's federal income tax from your current-year federal income tax.

Real estate taxes are those paid on real property of which you are the owner or co-owner. If you pay realty taxes on property that you do not own, the payments are disallowed. Legal "ownership" is the kind of thing an auditor is looking for here.

Personal property taxes include "registration fees" which are based on the value of tangible assets that you own, or those under your direct custody and care. These "fee" taxes apply to autos, trucks, boats, airplanes, machinery, equipment, and the like. Operating licenses are excluded.

Other than matters of ownership, year of payment(s), and excluded taxes, deductible taxes are rather straightforward.

Mortgage Interest "Matching"

One item on Schedule A which is not so straightforward has to do with home mortgage interest. For most middle-income taxpayers, mortgage interest is probably the highest single deduction on a tax return. For years, this right to deduct mortgage interest went unchallenged. Then in 1989 — with the blessing of Congress — the IRS came up with new gimmickry. It's all in Section 163 (Interest). That is, if you want to read its 6,000+ words!

Instead of home mortgage interest which everyone understood, it is now called *Qualified Residence Interest*. The term "qualified residence" is the principal residence of the taxpayer **plus one other** selected by the taxpayer as such. In other words, a "second residence" whether occupied or not counts, so long as it is not rented out for production-of-income purposes.

Subsection 163(h)(3)(A)(i) and (ii) goes on to state, in part, that—

The term "qualified residence interest" means any interest which is paid or incurred during the taxable year on—
  *(i)   **acquisition indebtedness** with respect to any qualified residence of the taxpayer, or*
  *(ii) **home equity indebtedness** with respect to any qualified residence of the taxpayer.* [Emphasis added.]

The term "acquisition indebtedness" is any kind of mortgage debt which—

  (i)   is incurred in acquiring, constructing, or substantially improving any qualified residence;
  (ii) is secured by such residence; and
  (iii) does not exceed $1,000,000 in the aggregate amount

The term "home equity indebtedness" is any kind of refinancing that does not exceed $100,000 [Sec. 163(h)(3)(B) and (C)]. In other words, there is now a deduction limit to one's home mortgage interest. It is that interest paid on one's **initial** acquisition indebtedness (up to $1,000,000) . . . **plus** up to $100,000 additional refinancing.

If you look at Schedule A, the "Interest You Paid" portion thereof, you will find the following lead-off entry:

Home mortgage interest and points reported to you on **Form 1098.** [Emphasis added.]

Right away, you see another form mentioned, namely: Form 1098 — Mortgage Interest Statement. This form is prepared by the mortgage company to whom you made your house payments. The form lists the company's Federal ID number, your social security number, your loan account number, and the amount of interest received from you.

The master copy of Form 1098 goes to the IRS's National Computer Center at Martinsburg, West Virginia. Here's where all the fun — and torture — begins.

Can you not imagine the computer-matching screwups that can and do occur? We tried to forewarn you of this in Chapter 7.

Mortgage companies these days buy each other out, reorganize, go bankrupt, or sell their loan accounts to others for collection. Homeowners buy and sell with mortgage "wraparounds." Married owners buy, split up, and remarry other owners. Family members (parents, children, brothers, sisters) arrange "equity sharing" deals among themselves. Multiple owners buy, live in, and make different mortgage payment arrangements. There are "second" mortgages and "third" mortgages; there are refinanced mortgages, line-of-credit mortgages, and mixed-use mortgages. All mortgage accounts, of whatever form and in whosoever's name (and social security number) are reported to the IRS on Form 1098 for its computer matching mania.

The matching problems for which we are trying to alert you are depicted in Figure 8.3. We just want you to be aware that the correct home mortgage interest amount deductible on Schedule A is no longer the simple matter that it once was. If there are any computer discrepancies, *you* will have to straighten them out. Otherwise, the auditor takes the easy course: he/she automatically disallows whatever you enter.

Other Interest Deductions

The Form 1098 computer matching requirement pertains only to that mortgage interest paid to financial institutions. If you make mortgage payments to other than financial institutions — friends, relatives, investors, homesellers — there is a separate line on Schedule A for you. The "other" line reads—

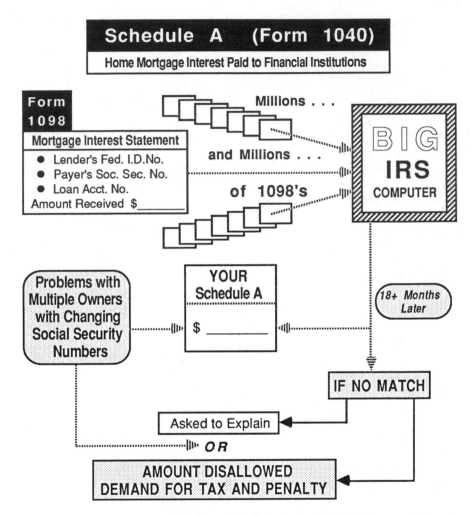

Fig. 8.3 - Computer Matching "Headache" with Mortgage Interest

Home mortgage interest not reported to you on Form 1098. If paid to the person from whom you bought the home, show that person's name, address, and identifying number.

You may have to communicate with the recipient (lender) to make sure that your interest amount corresponds with that which he is reporting as interest income on his tax return. In the process, you might as well request his social security number also. An aggressive auditor might insist that you produce some written confirmation from the lending person.

Another interest-paid line on Schedule A reads—

Points not reported to you on Form 1098. See [Instructions] *for special rules.*

The instructions tell you that "points," including loan origination and refinance fees, are generally deductible over the life of your mortgage. The exception is when you use the loan proceeds to **buy, build, or improve** your main home: NOT your "second" home. If you buy, build, or improve, the points and fees you pay for that money are deductible in the applicable year. Otherwise, you have to amortize (stretch out) the points and fees over a period of 15 to 30 years. This means that each year you have to keep a running tally. Have you done this?

Below the deductible points line is another line which reads—

Investment interest. If required, attach Form 4952.

Form 4952 is another detailed form with its own instructions. Its essence is that if you borrowed money for the acquisition of property (real, tangible, intangible) for investment purposes, you can deduct that investment interest to the extent of your investment income for the taxable year. Investment income is that which you receive in the form of interest, dividends, passive income (from partnerships, S corporations, estates, trusts, and rental real estate activities), and capital gains.

Now, for our teaser question.

You bought a parcel of land with the intention, someday, of building a home on it. You pay market-rate interest to the seller who is not a financial institution. What kind of interest have you paid: mortgage, investment, or personal?

Be careful how you characterize said interest. If it can be classed as personal interest by the auditor, you'll get no deduction for it. None whatsoever.

Disaster Loss "Carryback"

When we discussed casualty and theft loss deductions above, we purposely omitted telling you about disaster losses. The two loss categories are quite different. A casualty or theft loss tends to be more individualized. It is a one-victim situation. In contrast, a disaster loss is a many-victim situation. Consequently, different allowability rules apply.

A disaster is the widespread suffering and loss in an area subsequently determined by the President to warrant Federal assistance under the Disaster Relief and Emergency Assistance Act. In 1994, for example, there were 28 disaster areas proclaimed in the United States. They all derived from natural causes: tornadoes, severe freezing, severe flooding, earthquakes, hurricanes, severe thunderstorms, heavy rains, flash floods, severe mudslides, forest fires (caused by lightning), and the like.

In a proclaimed disaster area, an affected taxpayer may elect to take the deduction for his losses on his tax return for the year *immediately preceding* the taxable year in which the disaster occurred. This is called the disaster "carryback" election. If one paid substantially higher taxes in the prior year, this is an opportunity to get a **refund** of some or all of those taxes paid. The authority for this election is embodied in Section 165(i) of the tax code and its paragraphs (1) [deduction for preceding year], (2) [year of loss], and (3) [amount of loss].

The procedures for making the election are set forth in Regulation 1.165-11. In brief, the election can be made on or before **the later of** (1) the due date of the return for the year in which the disaster occurred, or (2) the due date of the preceding year's return, taking into account any extensions of time granted. One can make the election on his regular return, on an amended return, or on a claim for refund, provided he cites clearly thereon: Section 165(i). One still has to file Form 4684 (as in Figure 8.2) to compute the amount of deductible loss.

As subsection 165(i)(3) says—

*The amount of the loss taken into account in the preceding taxable year . . . shall not exceed the uncompensated amount determined on the basis of the **facts existing at the date** the taxpayer claims the loss.* [Emphasis added.]

There is a two-fold purpose behind the emphasized phrase: "facts existing," etc. A taxpayer cannot amend or reamend his return later to claim a higher loss. An overzealous auditor who enters the scene two, three, or more years later, cannot reinvent the facts to satisfy his revenue quota. Disaster loss computations and their relevant facts are quite complicated. They are made more so by the fact that clear and convincing evidence has itself been destroyed by the disaster.

So, document all the facts that you can when you prepare Form 4684. Even go so far as to *date the form* in the white space in its upper right-hand corner. Below the date, make the notation: **Sec. 165(i)(3) Election**. The IRS computer processing operators will not pick this up (it has no official line number), but you can point it out to the auditor. It is also good practice to hand-print in red the capitalized words: DISASTER AREA, in the available white space at Line 1 (on Form 4684).

Unreimbursed Employee Expenses

The next-to-last itemized category on Schedule A is captioned: Job Expenses and Most Other Miscellaneous Deductions. This category comprises two subparts, namely: (a) unreimbursed employee business expenses, and (b) most other unreimbursed expenses. The total of both subparts is subject to the 2% AGI floor mentioned earlier in this chapter.

The very first entry in this 2% AGI category is intended for job travel, union dues, job education, etc. Right on Schedule A, it says—

If required, you MUST attach Form 2106 or 2106-EZ [Employee Business Expenses].

Form 2106 (or 2106-EZ) is required if you are claiming any travel, transportation, meal, or entertainment generally exceeding $1,000 over the amount that you are reimbursed (if any). This form and its instructions provide numerous lines (about 40 in all) and adequate space for including all possible types of business expenses incurred by you on behalf of your employer. The Schedule A itself only provides two lines for this information.

The "most other" expenses portion of this 2% AGI category pertains to fees to employment agencies, certain legal and accounting fees, clerical help, office rent, and certain other not-for-profit type business expenses.

Once your grand total unreimbursed miscellaneous expenses exceed the 2% AGI threshhold, go back and "massage" your numbers. Discipline yourself to search for and recollect the maximum possible deduction benefits. To do this, carefully review the instructions to Schedule A and the instructions to Form 2106.

Put down as much detail as you can, and prepare and line up your receipts, records, diaries, mileage logs, and other documentation. This is one area where every IRS auditor thinks that he or she has an easy win. Make the auditor work as much as you had to work to prepare for the audit.

Other Miscellaneous Deductions

At the beginning of this chapter, we said that there were approximately 25 line entries on Schedule A. The actual official number of lines may vary by one or two, from year to year. This is why in our discussion above, we did not follow the official listing sequence. We wanted you to get the substance of the deduction, rather than worrying about where it went on the form.

To put the Schedule A deductions in their official sequence, we present Figure 8.4. We, of course, have edited, simplified, and emphasized the key features of each deduction item. Particularly note that we have not used official line numbers. It is the deduction sequence as shown numerically that we want you to be aware of. You can use Figure 8.4 as a quick check-off list for assuring yourself that you haven't missed anything.

Caution: When you enter a deductible item on your own tax return, be sure to match it to the correct official line number. These line numbers change from year to year; so, be careful. A correct amount entered on an incorrect line number will cause "red flagging." This alone may up your DIF score that we talked about in Chapter 2.

And, as always on most tax forms, there is one final catchall line on Schedule A. The very last line entry before total deductions reads—

Other miscellaneous deductions. List type and amount.

These other deductions are those which are not subject to the 2% AGI threshold. They are "other" in the sense that they are not everyday-type events. But they are deductible nevertheless.

The official instructions for these deductions read—

Use this line to report miscellaneous deductions that are NOT subject to the 2% AGI limit. Only the expenses listed below can be deducted:

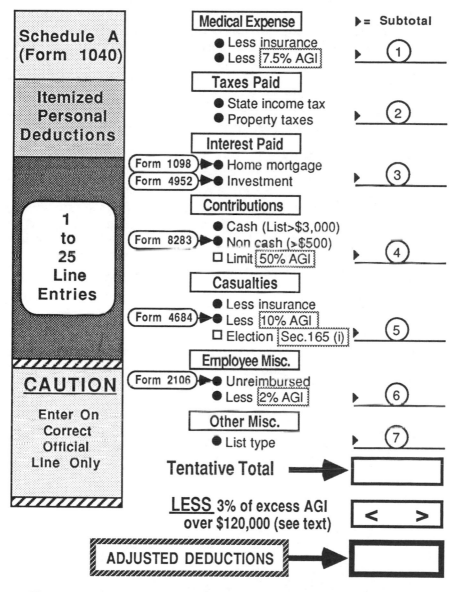

Fig. 8.4 - The Sequence of Deduction Entries on Schedule A

• Gambling losses (to the extent of winnings).
• Certain income tax on estates.
• Amortization of certain bond premiums.

• Repayment of claims over $3,000.
• Unrecovered investment in a pension.
• Impairment-related work expenses of a disabled person.

If you make an entry on this last line, be sure to identify it with one or more of these six items. Even then, your entry will be audit challenged. So, prepare a statement referencing the exact wording in the official instructions, and attach it to your return.

New Phase-Out Rule

The IRS gimmick designers never stop. They'd like nothing better than eliminating Schedule A entirely. Always bellyaching how overworked they are, the IRS in 1990 persuaded Congress to enact another new gimmick law, Section 68: *Overall Limitation on Itemized Deductions*. More generally, this is referred to as the 3% phase-out rule. It applies only to taxpayers whose AGI exceeds $100,000.

Section 68(a) reads in essential part as—

In the case of an individual whose adjusted gross income [AGI] *exceeds the applicable amount, the amount of the itemized deductions* [on Schedule A] *otherwise allowable . . . shall be reduced by the lesser of—*

(i) 3 percent of the excess of AGI over the applicable amount, or
(ii) 80 percent of the amount of the itemized deductions otherwise allowable.

Section 68(b) defines "applicable amount" as $100,000 indexed for inflation, for years after 1990. For example, in 1994 the applicable amount was $111,800; in 1996, it was $117,950.

We've already called your attention to the 3% "lesser of" reduction in Figure 8.4. This 3% reduction is not something that you can audit prepare for. However, it should put you on notice that the auditor will drive up your AGI as high as possible, before he/she tackles your Schedule A deduction items. All of this booby-trapping with AGI thresholds should irritate you to the point of trying harder to claim all bona fide Schedule A items that you can.

9

SCHEDULE C ITEMS

A Schedule C Filer Is Usually A Self-Employed Person Pursuing Actively A Trade, Business, Or Profession. His/Her First Phase Of Audit Comprises Those Painful Steps From Gross Receipts To Gross Income. Preparatory Presentation Includes All Bank Statements, Billing Invoices, Returns And Allowances, Cost Of Goods And/Or Services, Ending Inventory, And "Other Income." From Gross Income, All "Ordinary And Necessary" Business Expenses Are Allowable. In This Phase, Audit Focus Is On Personal Expenses, Mixed-Use Items, And Documentation Of "More Than 50%" Business Use. The Audit Is Simplified When Using Straight-Line-Only Depreciation.

Schedule C (Form 1040) is officially titled: **Profit or Loss From Business (Sole Proprietorship)**. This schedule is used by persons who are self-employed, who engage in activities for which their compensation is by invoicings and billings to their customers and clients. As such, their compensation is not reported to the IRS in the same way that employee earnings are reported on Form W-2: Wage and Tax Statement. Immediately, this makes Schedule C filers tax suspect.

Roughly, there are about 25,000,000 (25 million) Schedule C filers each year. Many of these, however, involve part-time side ventures and not-for-profit activities. Such "businesses" are characterized by relatively low income, with expense deductions significantly exceeding the income. This inevitably produces a bottom-line loss. This loss can be used to offset positive sources of income, such as W-2 wages, for example. These kinds of Schedule C are **not** our focus in this chapter.

We are concerned herein with the proprietor who is making a living — or trying to — by the active conduct of his trade, business, or profession. This is the *material participation* test which characterizes the applicable Schedule C as a "business audit." If you are self-employed, or essentially so, you'll be subjected to more severe tax accounting procedures than for Schedule A.

Size and Audit Likelihood

The "size" of a Schedule C business is measured by its gross receipts. One's gross receipts are the starting amount from which all business deductions are allowed. The deductions include returns and allowances, cost of goods, cost of services, and other off-the-top adjustments.

A taxpayer/auditee may operate one business full-time, or he may operate several businesses part-time. If the aggregate of his business (or businesses) exceeds $100,000, he is virtually "guaranteed" to be audited within the next three to five years. This is because, since 1982, greater audit attention is being given to successful small businesses than in the past. The IRS figures that any sole proprietorship grossing over $100,000 is more likely than not engaged in attempting to claim more deductions than the owner can justify.

In the tax-audit world, a "small" business is one which grosses less than $1,000,000. Characteristically, small businesses do not employ full-time bookkeepers and accountants. The owner is preoccupied with trying to keep his business alive. Recordkeeping for tax purposes is not his most pressing concern. Consequently, small businesses become natural targets for aggression by the IRS. Its auditors sense an easy "kill."

Large corporations, on the other hand, have highly skilled attorneys and accountants on their staff. These corporate staffers often can out-wit and out-match any IRS audit team. Therefore, the IRS is more cautious in attacking large businesses.

From the gross income of a business, operating expenses are deducted to arrive at net earnings. The ratio of net earnings to gross income is a characterization index which the IRS notes. After many years of auditing small businesses, it has developed a catalog of profit profiles for proprietorship businesses. If your "profit profile" is below the norm, chances are you will be audited.

If a small business operates at a loss for three years in a row, audit is guaranteed. How can one operate at a loss for three or more years and still stay in business? Has the owner a substantial cache of unreported income?

Gross Income Verification

The very first thing that a Schedule C auditor will do is spend two to three hours, at least, digging through and verifying your gross income. Right off the bat he'll want you to produce ALL of your bank statements. He wants your business bank statements; he wants your personal bank statements; he wants your investment account statements; he wants your savings account passbooks; and he wants every bank, savings, or financial account of your *dependents* whom you may have listed on Form 1040. Never mind your financial privacy. You've got to lay it all out on the table. If the audit year is 1997, for example, you've got to produce monthly statements commencing December 1996 and going through January 1998. That's a total of 14 monthly statements for each account!

If you object in any way, no matter how courteous or diplomatic you try to be, your objection will be interpreted as though you were trying to hide something. And if you dare mention the words "Constitution" or "Constitutional Rights," you are automatically suspected of tax evasion . . . or of being a tax protester.

So, prepare for the worst. Go back and review Chapter 5: Income Verification. Track through *all* of your bank deposits for the audit year. Know or trail where each one originated. If money that went into your personal or investment derived from your business, make sure that it went into your business account first. Take a moment now to go back and review Figure 5.2 (on page 5-14).

If you pass the bank accounts grilling, the next suspicious target is your invoices and billings to your customers and clients. This is your "accounts receivable" . . . or whatever system you keep. How does the auditor otherwise know? You could have billed a person, received the money, and tucked it in your pocket. No bank deposit would show this.

If your total (business) bank deposits, billings, and gross receipts reported on Schedule C are within approximately five percent of each other, the auditor will go on to the next phase.

Returns and Allowances, Etc.

The next verification phase is your returns and allowances, cost of goods and services (your "direct costs"), and other incidental income for which you have no invoices or billings. If you pass the gross verification phase, this phase can go quite quickly.

All proper *returns and allowances* are the first deductibles from your gross receipts. These are such items as bounced checks which you deposited, refunds or discounts that you gave your clients, merchandise that you took back and restocked in inventory, sales taxes included in gross receipts (you don't want to pay income tax on your sales tax collections, do you?) and other adjustments.

Other income which is not of depository form or subject to ordinary billing consists of petty cash, scrap sales, barter exchanges, interest on personal loans, tax and insurance refunds, prizes and awards, honorarium fees, and depreciation recapture. Usually, there's not much documentation on these items. As a result, the auditor will probably ask some pointed questions and you can answer any way you choose. Before answering, however, you should understand the nomenclature that he is dealing with.

As to nomenclature, we have used rather interchangeably the terms "gross receipts" and "gross income." They are not the same. There is a sequence of events from one to the other. We present this sequence in Figure 9.1. Each sequential step along the way is a separate audit issue. No auditor will go beyond gross income until he or she is satisfied that your disclosures on Schedule C are within the normal bounds of accounting accuracy.

Cost of Goods & Services

One item of particular note in Figure 9.1 is "Cost of goods and/or services sold": item 4. The correct official term is *Cost of Goods Sold*. This term is not always self-evident, especially for businesses which are professional or service oriented. The term "goods sold" implies a business where merchandise is bought wholesale and sold at retail. It also implies a manufacturing business where parts and raw materials are fabricated into finished products which are sold at wholesale, retail, or both.

But what about real estate sales agents and insurance brokers? What about attorneys, doctors, accountants, and consultants? What about manufacturers' reps, commission salespersons, construction-

Phase I - INCOME	Schedule C : Sole Proprietorship	
Sequence	**Item (PRODUCE RECORDS)**	**Amount**
1.	GROSS RECEIPTS or sales ▶	$
2.	Returns and allowances	$
3.	<u>SUBTRACT</u> Item 2 from Item 1	$
4.	Cost of goods and/or services SOLD (from Part III, Sch.C : Fig. 9.2)	$
5.	<u>SUBTRACT</u> Item 4 from Item 3	$
6.	Other income (not in Item 1) ▶	$
7.	<u>ADD</u> Items 5 and 6 **This is your GROSS INCOME** ▶	////////

Fig. 9.1 - Audit Sequence from Gross Receipts to Gross Income

industry contractors, and horticulturists? All of these occupations have **direct costs** which are analogous to cost of goods sold.

If properly classified and identified, all direct costs become a *subtraction* — usually a major one — from gross receipts before arriving at gross income. The items of direct cost to be identified are set forth in Part III of Schedule C. This is a separate subschedule of its own and is miniaturized in Figure 9.2. This figure is to assist you in identifying those officially recognized direct-cost items, when the auditor asks for your records therewith. If you have any entries in Part III, you can be sure that the large dollar-amount items will be scrutinized first. Large subtraction amounts always attract an auditor's attention.

The term "purchases" applies to all acquisitions of merchandise (finished or semi-finished) which you stock in inventory for resale. Your best evidence of these purchases is your supplier invoices which you should have kept in a separate file of their own. Depending on whether you are on a cash or accrual basis, you should have each supplier invoice backed up with one or more cancelled checks or credit memos. Generally, there is no audit problem here, if you are systematic and keep organized records.

Part III	Schedule C (page 2)		
COST OF GOODS AND SERVICES SOLD		/////////	
1 .	Inventory : Beginning of year	1 .	
2 .	Purchases for resale	2 .	
3 .	Materials and supplies	3 .	
4 .	Cost of labor	4 .	
5 .	Other costs (explain)	5 .	
6 .	Subtotal : ADD lines 1 through 5	6 .	
7 .	Inventory : End of year	7 .	
8 .	SUBTRACT line 7 from line 6 and enter on designated income line	8 .	▼ ▼ ▼ ▼
/////	COST OF GOODS AND SERVICES SOLD	▶	

Fig. 9.2 - Cost of Goods/Services Sold to Customers/Clients

The item labeled "cost of labor" (in Figure 9.2) is a real bear trap. This means W-2-type labor only: **not** outside vendors or independent contractors. Any entry here means that you are an employer, with regular payroll to meet. Be prepared to show your payroll ledgers, your employer quarterly returns (Forms 941), the W-2s that you prepared, the W-4s (Withholding Allowances) that your employees prepared, and your Federal tax deposit receipts (Forms 8109). Be extra careful that you do not include any vendors or contractors. If you trip up on this one, you'll learn first-hand why we are warning you.

There are parts, raw materials, and shop supplies for the finishing, storing, and shipping of your line of products or services. This item may even include small tools if consumable in nature, or of the type subject to damage or carting off inadvertently. Again, all you need are your supplier billings, cash receipts, and similar evidence of purchase.

The catchall category of your direct costs is just simply "Other costs (explain)." These are such costs as—

- freight in
- fees and permits
- pickup and delivery services
- outside vendors
- independent contractors
- subcontractors
- printing and photography
- capitalized expenses

Most of these are not large-dollar items. Therefore, an experienced auditor will skim through your listings and documentation to see if they are properly capitalized. But if you have any independent contractors, we guarantee you that he will pick on those.

Independent Contractors: 1099s

An independent contractor is a person who is not on your regular payroll. He performs specific contractual tasks to be performed within a specific time frame. He is "in business for himself," so to speak. He comes and goes as he pleases, uses his own tools, has his own place of business, has his own transportation and equipment, places his own insurance, and pays his own taxes. He doesn't get paid until he completes the contracted job. He is not subject to withholdings by you in any form. For this reason, he is a *nonemployee*.

There is one key distinction between an employee and nonemployee (independent contractor). Upon completion of each contracted task, the independent contractor submits to you an invoice billing. It gives a description of the job performed, hours, dates, and so forth. In other words, he submits to you an invoice just like any other supplier or vendor. He does this irregularly throughout the year. Presumably, he contracts with other business persons than yourself. He may be a technician, consultant, tradesman, or other form of free lancer. Whatever you do, be sure to save all of the invoices on which you pay. The auditor is going to want to see every one of those invoices.

If you pay $600 or more during the taxable year to any contracting person, you become a payer-reporter to the IRS. You do this by filing an "information return" known as **Form 1099-MISC** (Miscellaneous Income). There is a special box thereon labeled: *Nonemployee compensation.*

If you engage one or more independent contractors, you'd better become familiar with Form 1099-MISC. To assist you in this regard, we present an edited and abridged version of this form in Figure 9.3. You need to display your own Federal ID number and,

PAYER Name & Address	1.	FORM 1099 - MISC
	2.	Statement for recipients of Miscellaneous Income
	3.	
Payer's Fed. I.D. No.	Payee's Soc. Sec. No.	4. Federal tax withheld
PAYEE Name & Address	5.	6.
	7. Nonemployee compensation	8.
	9.	
Copy A : for IRS	Copy 2 : for State	Copy B : for Payee	Copy C : for Payer

Fig. 9.3 - Edited Version of Form 1099 for Nonemployees

of course — as always — the social security number of the recipient contractor (or other payee).

What if you paid several independent contractors and didn't report each amount on a separate 1099? This is where the auditor has you where he wants you.

First: All of your independent contractor payments will be disallowed. This will decrease your cost of goods and/or services . . . and *increase* your tax.

Second: The auditor will recommend imposition of the $50 penalty for *each* 1099 failure.

Third: The auditor will start looking more closely for other 1099s that you should have filed, such as for rents, royalties, prizes and awards, expense reimbursements, substitute payments, barter, and so forth.

If you complain too hostilely about all of the added paperwork, the auditor may quote to you Section 6723: *Failure to Comply with Other Information Reporting Requirements*. This section reads in full as—

In the case of a failure by any person to comply with a specified information reporting requirement on or before the time prescribed therefor, such person shall pay a penalty of $50 for each such failure, but the total amount imposed on such person *for all such failures during any calendar year shall not exceed $100,000.*

When the auditor reads the $100,000 maximum penalty bit, you'll get the message. You'll also rush to the nearest IRS office and request **Package 1099**: Instructions to Filers of Forms 1099, 1098, 5498, 1096, and W-2G.

Ending Inventory: Sec. 263A

Another paperwork matter has to do with ending inventory (in Figure 9.2). Most Schedule C filers know and understand the direct costs that are tied up in ending inventory. But they do not understand or accept as reasonable the host of indirect costs that also must be included in inventory. This is where Section 263A comes in: *Capitalization and Inclusion in Inventory Costs of Certain Expenses.*

Section 263A is one of the most vexatious tax laws that the IRS has forced upon small businesses. It requires you to capitalize all *allocable costs* with respect to any real or tangible personal property produced by a Schedule C filer. These so-called "allocable costs" are ordinary expense items such as taxes, interest, insurance, advertising, contract negotiations, inspections, appraisals, repairs, utilities, rent, warehousing, and so on. The IRS lists in its Regulation 1.263A-1(e)(3)(ii) some 25 of these allocable cost items. The allocation procedures proposed by the IRS are truly an accounting nightmare.

Section 263(A)(a) reads in selected part—

Nondeductibility of certain direct and indirect costs:
- *In the case of property which is inventory in the hand of the taxpayer* [it] *shall be included in inventory costs.*
- *In the case of any other property,* [the allocable costs] *shall be capitalized.*
- *Allocable costs . . . are the direct costs of such property, and such property's proper share of those indirect costs (including taxes) part or all of which are allocable to such property.*

We forewarned you about Section 263A — its 2,500 statutory words and its 150,000 regulatory words — in the latter part of Chapter 6. Fortunately (and we do mean fortunately), this "capitalization-inclusion" rule is so utterly complex and confusing that most IRS auditors themselves are bewildered and confused by it. There are special exception clauses such as subsections 263A(b), (c), and (h). Regulation 1.263A-1(b)(12) is particularly pertinent. This is the *de minimis rule* for producers and resellers whose total indirect costs are $200,000 or less. There are other de minimis rules for producers whose gross receipts are $1,000,000 or less, and resellers whose gross receipts are $10,000,000 or less. Consequently, for a "small business," any reasonable good-faith inventory accounting is likely to be accepted.

"Ordinary and Necessary": Sec. 162

Up to this point, we have taken you from gross receipts to gross income . . . as per Figure 9.1. Of all Schedule C auditing procedures, the gross income phase is the most painful. It interferes with and distorts your rationale and purpose of being in business. From this point on, however, deductible business expenses are more straightforward and understandable.

The "father law" of deductible business expenses is Section 162: *Trade or Business Expenses*. The general rule therewith is subsection (a), to wit—

> *There shall be allowed as a deduction all the **ordinary and necessary** expenses paid or incurred during the taxable year in carrying on any trade or business, including . . .* [Emphasis added.]

Then some 18 subsections follow.

A more comprehensive statement of this general rule is found in Regulation 1.162-1(a): *Business Expenses; In General*. Pertinent portions of this regulation are—

> *Business expenses deductible from gross income include the ordinary and necessary expenditures directly connected with or pertaining to the taxpayer's trade or business. . . . Among the items included in business expenses are management expenses, commissions, labor, supplies, incidental repairs, operating expenses of automobiles, traveling expenses, advertising and other selling expenses, together with insurance premiums against . . . losses, and* [the] *rental . . . of business property . . . . The full amount of the allowable deduction for ordinary*

and necessary expenses in carrying on a business is deductible, even though such expenses exceed the gross income derived during the taxable year from such business.

On its surface, Regulation 1.162-1(a) is reasonably clear. The problem is one of interpretation. Most IRS auditors have never been in business for themselves. They have genuine difficulty in comprehending what is "ordinary and necessary" for every business that they audit. Interpreting the word "supplies" is a good illustration.

Recently a real estate agent was audited. He had deducted as supplies a $369 item invoiced to him as linoleum. The auditor disallowed the $369 based on her conjecture that the linoleum was for the taxpayer's kitchen in his own home. She had just put in some linoleum in her kitchen, so she knew. Or did she?

As it turned out, in order to close the sale on a 4-plex residence, the agent/auditee had to replace $369 worth of hallway linoleum. The buyer was adamant. The auditee stood to lose $5,620 in (taxable) realty commissions. So, the agent paid for the replacement linoleum himself. It was a *necessary* expense to get his commission; it may not have been ordinary. Headstrong auditors do not always recognize these distinctions.

Exceptions Under Sec. 162

The general rule of Section 162 does not allow all expenses, even though they may be ordinary and necessary in the course of one's business. There are three specific exceptions (for Schedule C filers) that we must tell you about.

Most businesses are faced with sporadic requests for donations of money and/or gifts of property for charitable and worthy causes. Many businesses make such contributions as a matter of humane policy and good public relations. But such donations are *not* deductible business expenses. They are treated as personal deductions, subject to other conditions and limitations.

Subsection 162(b) specifically states—

No deduction shall be allowed under subsection (a) for any contribution or gift which would be allowable under section 170 [relating to itemized personal deductions].

Even though not deductible as business expenses, many donations are paid out of business funds, simply because the owner is approached during business hours or on business premises. If the donated amounts are not too great, they could be included under "advertising and promotion." But they are not supposed to be.

Another exception has to do with illegal payments: bribes, kickbacks, referral fees, payoffs, and rebates. These items are detailed in subsection 162(c) under the sub-subheadings of—

(1) Illegal payments to government officials or employees.
(2) Illegal payments to unlicensed go-betweens.
(3) Kickbacks and rebates under medicare and medicaid.

As a group, bribes and kickbacks are classed as payments in *frustration of public policy*. Almost every form of business offers some kind of "courtesy fee" for the referral of a client, patient, customer, or contract. Unless carried to the extreme, these referral fees are justified. An owner can pay a commission to his designated agent. So, why can't he pay a gratuitous fee to an incidental, voluntary agent?

Because of the generally accepted practice of paying (or crediting) gratuities for business, any allegation of illegal payment must be proven by the IRS. That is, under subsection 162(c), the burden of proof is on the IRS to establish that a payment is indeed illegal under applicable federal and state laws. The IRS is not known for accepting *its own* burden of proof gracefully.

One very clear disallowance pertains to fines and penalties. On this point, subsection 162(f) is specific:

> *No deduction shall be allowed under subsection (a) for any fine or similar penalty paid to a government for the violation of any law.*

Typical such items are traffic tickets and tax penalties. They are not deductible no matter how directly connected they are to one's trade or business.

Overview of the Deductions

Except for the three exceptions above, Section 162 is quite clear. Verifiable ordinary and necessary expenditures *shall be allowed*. Because of this deduction specificity, small business tax schedules are preprinted with certain allowable deductions thereon. A listing of these deductions on Schedule C (Form 1040) is presented in Figure 9.4.

Be aware, of course, that the item numbers in Figure 9.4 do not correspond with the line numbers on the official tax forms. The *sequence*, however, is correct. For its own computer convenience, the IRS keeps changing the official line numbers.

Form 1040	SCHEDULE C	Tax Year
	TRADE, BUSINESS, PROFESSION	

BUSINESS DESCRIPTION AND INCOME SOURCES

GROSS INCOME_____

DEDUCTIONS

1. Advertising	15. Repairs
2. Bad debts	16. Supplies, other
3. Car & truck expenses	17. Taxes
4. Commissions paid	18. Travel & lodging
5. Depletion	19. Meals & entertainment
6. Depreciation **(Form 4562)**	a. 100% M&E b. enter 50% of above
7. Employee benefits	c. subtract the 50%
8. Freight & shipping	20. Phone & utilities
9. Insurance	21. Wages paid
10. Interest paid • Mortgage • Other	22. Other expenses a._____
11. Legal & professional	b._____
12. Office expense	c._____
13. Pension & profit sharing plans	d._____
14. Rent paid • Machinery & equip. • Other	e._____ f._____

Fig. 9.4 - Edited Deductions Preprinted on Schedule C (1040)

We urge you to read through Figure 9.4 carefully. It will give you a good overview of the types of business deductions that are readily allowable. Some items are self-explanatory; others are not.

For example, one of the most commonly misunderstood deductions is "bad debts." Tax-deductionwise, the term bad debt means that you have included in gross income money which you have not received and will not receive. If you have reported an amount in gross income, and never, ever receive that amount, you get a bad debt deduction.

Suppose you properly reported an $800 billing in gross income, either in the current year or in some prior year. Despite vigorous efforts to collect this $800, you are unable to do so. You have a bad debt. But if the $800 was never reported as income, you have no bad debt. You have less gross income by the amount of $800 uncollected.

The item "pension and profit-sharing plans" is also misleading. It does not include contributions to said plan(s) by the owner of the business. He gets his deduction elsewhere on Form 1040, but not on Schedule C. This item is strictly for contributions made on behalf of employees. "Employee benefit programs" comprise your expenses for food, coffee, snacks, prizes, awards, and promotional gifts on premises to your employees. Caution: do not include similar expenditures for independent contractors. Use Form 1099-MISC instead.

The item "taxes" requires a separate subitemization of its own. It does not include any income tax payable by the owner. This deduction is intended for sales taxes, property taxes, payroll taxes, licenses, permits, assessments, and other compulsory payments levied upon the business itself, as opposed to being levied personally upon the owner.

By all means, take care to note in Figure 9.4 the entry labeled: "Meals & entertainment." This is the disallowance routine that auditors love to beat you over the head with. By showing it on Schedule C, it is intended to impress upon you the fact that you must first reduce M & E by 50% before any is deductible.

Line Item Packaging

Now, for some worldly advice. If *your* Schedule C is being audited, be prepared to substantiate *every* deduction item, line by line, for which you have made an entry. Be prepared for every line, whether an auditor specifically requests this of you or not.

On Schedule C audits, IRS auditors have a habit of changing their minds as they proceed along the listed deductions in Figure 9.4. For example, an auditor may have indicated to you by phone or in writing that he wants to see primarily your documentation of advertising and storage/warehousing expenses. Weeks (and months) later, at audit, you can't count on him sticking to his word. If you rely on it, and resist going beyond it, he will simply take out his official "Request for Information" pad and write down every line item on Schedule C. So, go in fully prepared.

The best way to do this is to package all of your documentation separately for each line item. If you have made 15 line entries, for example, you should have 15 separate packages. Within each package, *circle in red* the expense figure on each document. Then, for each package, run an adding machine tape on all expenditures that are red penciled. Attach the tape to its respective line item package. Identify each package by the official line number on your tax form. Arrange all packages in their official line number sequence on their return.

If one or more of your line item packages tallies in excess of that which you initially entered on your return, that's fine. Since you have it documented, claim it. If a package or two tallies less than what you entered on the schedule, concede it. Don't get rattled simply because you cannot match everything dollar-for-dollar, or penny-for-penny. Auditors expect some inconsistencies two or three years after a return is filed. It is the bottom line of *total deductions* that you want to come reasonably close.

Most auditors are surprised when a Schedule C auditee comes in with each line entry supported by a neat package of documents of its own. If you are this well prepared, lay your packages out sequentially so that the auditor can see them. Without saying so, you are implying that the auditor can take his (or her) pick.

Seeing your preparedness, the auditor will ask first for one line item. Suppose this is "repairs" or "maintenance." You present the requested deduction item and let the auditor go through every document. Keep silent; volunteer no information. Let the auditor ask questions if he or she wants to. Chances are, the auditor will be preoccupied with matching the expenditures on each document with the entries on your adding machine tape. Or, he/she will read each document to see if it fulfills the "ordinary and necessary" requirement. The auditor will make notes on his/her worksheets.

After meticulously checking two or three of your line item packages, he/she will start skimming through the others. If you have 15 packages, for example, and the first random three are nearly perfect, the auditor will speed things up. He/she then wants to be satisfied that there are no duplications of expenditures, and that there is no padding with phony documents.

As long as your total deductions are within a few hundred dollars of those which you initially claimed, most auditors will accept the return-entered total and go on to the next matter.

Pick-Picking at Personal Use

Auditors are especially trained to be on the lookout for personal use expenditures on Schedule C. While you are presenting your line item packages, their eyes and ears are on "pick alert." That is, they will simply pick-pick away. Nothing is said to you until they have found a vulnerable spot.

Small businesses are particularly vulnerable to claiming personal expenses as business deductions. Sometimes there is honest confusion. But more often, carelessness and/or bravado gather momentum. This proceeds to the point where the distinction between personal and business becomes blurred.

Take the matter of insurance, for example. All business-necessitated insurance is deductible. This includes product liability, hazard insurance (to business property), errors and omissions, malpractice, workmen's compensation, performance bonds, and the like. This does *not* include insurance on your life, even if called "key man" insurance. Nor does it include collision insurance on your wife's car, nor medical insurance on your children.

The tax problem with insurance is that brokers and underwriters want to package all of your coverages into one statement. They allegedly give you some sort of multi-coverage discount for doing so. You must get *two* separate statements: one for your business affairs and one for your personal affairs. Unless you insist on two statements, or on two different insurance companies, the auditor has you over a barrel.

Another personal use area for pick-picking is car and truck expenses. Some auditors take the position that no highway vehicle can ever be 100% business used. They contend that it is highly unlikely that on your way to or from a business errand you never, ever stopped to pick up a quart of milk or a pack of cigarettes. If you ever did, they then insist on your producing a daily mileage log showing business miles and personal miles.

In one extreme case, an auditee substantiated (to the dollar) all of his car and truck expenses with gasoline receipts and repair bills. He was in the business of selling and installing greenhouses and solariums in private residences. He used a pickup truck with steel racks and bars for transporting tools, supplies, and panels. He had some 40 to 50 suppliers and customers. His business mileage easily exceeded 30,000 miles for the year. His stop-off personal mileage, if any, was less than 500 miles. Obviously, he kept no daily mileage log. He was too busy with customer problems.

Because the IRS audit manual says: *must have business mileage log*, the auditor was going to disallow all gas and repair expenses. Fortunately, the auditee had the presence of mind to say: "This is a *qualified nonpersonal use vehicle*: Section 174(i)." [The auditee was precoached on this, of course.] The auditor relented.

A nonpersonal use vehicle does not come under the same substantiation requirements of Section 274(d), as does a "mixed-use" vehicle. Specifically, Section 274(i) says—

For purposes of subsection (d), the term "qualified nonpersonal use vehicle" means any vehicle which, by reason of its nature, is not likely to be used more than a de minimis amount for personal purposes.

To help overcome car and truck audit problems, every person in business should have two vehicles: one vehicle for strictly business use; the other vehicle for strictly personal use. Never interchange the two (or at least never admit to interchanging).

The same recommendation applies to a telephone. When in business, have two phones (one business, one personal).

Go out of your way to separate out *any and all* personal use expenditures. If you don't, sooner or later you will be cornered.

1099-MISCs Revisited

Earlier, when discussing cost of goods and/or services, we introduced you to Form 1099-MISC (Figure 9.3). The focus at that time was on independent contractors. We cautioned you that if you missed preparing these "information returns" on those persons, the auditor would be looking elsewhere on your Schedule C where the 1099s could apply. We're talking now about boxes 1, 2, 3, 6, 8, and 9 in Figure 9.3.

That "elsewhere" is the entire field of expense deductions shown in Figure 9.4. In particular, the auditor will be picking at your documents for such matters as:

- Commissions paid
- Referral fees
- Professional fees
- Secretarial services
- Graphics and art

- Rents paid
- Interest paid
- Prizes and awards
- Computer services
- Maintenance services

Technically, a 1099-MISC is required for each person to whom you paid $600 or more. The exceptions are those persons to whom you make payments in the corporate form. That is, if your check is made out to a registered company name, rather to an individual name, no 1099 is required.

Otherwise, you are supposed to ask each payee for his or her SSN: Social Security Number. If a payee refuses to give, or dawdles too long in giving, his number, then you are supposed to withhold 30% of the gross amount due. To indicate this on Form 1099-MISC, you have to fill out Box 4: *Federal income tax withheld*. Then, naturally, you have to fill out more forms to turn the money over to the IRS. This puts you in the thankless and time-consuming position of being an IRS tax collector . . . without pay.

The 30% withholding routine is called "backup withholding." You are statutorily required to do this by virtue of Section 3406(a): *Requirement to Deduct and Withhold*. In pertinent part, this subsection reads—

In the case of any reportable payment, if the payee fails to furnish his SSN to the payer in the manner required, . . . then the payer shall deduct and withhold from such payment a tax equal to 30 percent of such payment.

Cover yourself by issuing to your payees **Form W-9**: *Request for Taxpayer Identification Number and Certification*. Have a batch of Forms W-9 handy at all times for this purpose. If a payee refuses to furnish his SSN, have said person sign the *Certification* that he is **not** subject to backup withholding. Then enter "Exempt" in the SSN space on Form 1099-MISC. Above all, do *not* withhold! Otherwise, you become hopelessly entangled in Section 3406 and its 38 subsections.

The Sec. 179 Expense Election

For small businesses, there is a special "expense election" when acquiring certain depreciable assets. As you probably already know, tangible property used in a trade or business is subject to a stretched-out allowance, called depreciation. This applies to such productive items as furniture and fixtures, computers and faxes, equipment and machinery, large tools, vehicles, and other nonrealty classed as recovery property. Section 179 permits a dollar-limited exception to the depreciation rules.

The full official heading of Section 179 is: *Election to Expense Certain Depreciable Business Assets.* Subsections (a) and (b) thereunder read:

(a) **Treatment as expenses**
A taxpayer may elect to treat the cost of any section 179 property as an expense which is not chargeable to capital account. Any cost so treated shall be allowed as a deduction for the taxable year in which the . . . property is placed in service.

(b) **Dollar limitation**
The aggregate cost which may be taken into account . . . shall not exceed the following applicable amount:

1996	*$17,500*	*2000*	*$20,000*
1997	*18,000*	*2001*	*24,000*
1998	*18,500*	*2002*	*24,000*
1999	*19,000*	*2003*	*25,000*

In other words, instead of depreciating certain items of business equipment, one may expense his aggregate cost up to $17,500/$25,000 (depending on year "placed in service"). There are three requirements for getting the deduction. The items must be:

(1) acquired by purchase,
(2) placed in service in a trade or business, and
(3) predominantly (over 50%) used for business.

Proving "acquired by purchase" can be established by presenting a purchase invoice or purchase contract.

Proving "placed in service" requires some verifiable first-incidence of actual use. If the item is a bench tool or instrument, for example, an under-penalty-of-perjury statement, dated, by the first person to use the item is helpful. If it is a computer for directing business activities, a copy of the first printout instructions, dated, is helpful. A shipping invoice showing the date that the equipment was delivered is not good enough. The delivered equipment could sit for weeks and months before being placed in service. The year of placement in service, even if for only one business day, entitles one to the entire $17,500/$25,000 expense deduction. Regulation 1.179-1(c) says that *proration is not required.*

Proving "predominant use in business" requires some kind of use and time log, or some other indication that personal use was not a factor. Property used exclusively at one's active place of business, which is not in his home or in his car, generally satisfies the "more than 50%" predominant use requirement. The term "predominant use" refers to the full 12 months of the "second taxable year" following the first taxable year of placement in service (Reg. 1.179-1(e)(1)). If not so used in the second year of service, the expensed amount is *recaptured.* That is, it is treated as other income on Schedule C for the recapture year.

Listed Property: Sec. 280F

Depreciable assets used in a small business always have been a target for audit attack. This is because certain types of tangible property lend themselves to "mixed-use": part business and part personal. Instead of calling it mixed-use property, it is now designated as *listed property.* The whole purpose of Section 280F is to target listed property and set special conditions for the deduction of any depreciation that may be claimed.

Subsection 280F(d)(4) designates the following depreciable items as listed property:

1. Any passenger automobile.
2. Any other property used as a means of transportation.
3. Any property of the type generally used for entertainment, recreation, or amusement.
4. Any computer or peripheral equipment.
5. Any cellular telephone or other similar telecommunication equipment.
6. Any other property that the IRS by regulation so designates.

Needless to say, the IRS has promulgated a whole raft of regulations: 1.280F-1T(a) through 1.280F-7T(b). These comprise

Form 4562	Depreciation and Amortization	Part III

LISTED PROPERTY	A. Depreciation B. Auto Mileage

1. Any evidence to support business use? ☐ yes ☐ no
2. If "yes", is evidence written? ☐ yes ☐ no
3. If auto(s) claimed, list following mileages:
   Business_____ ; Commute_____ ; Personal_____

4. Is another vehicle available for personal use? ☐ yes ☐ no

Entry Item	Property Used More Than 50%			Property Used 50% or Less	
(a) Type of property					
(b) Date in service					
(c) Business use %					
(d) Cost or other basis					
(e) Business use basis					
(f) Recovery period					
(g) Method used				S/L	S/L
(h) Depreciation deduction					
(i) Sec.179 election					

Fig. 9.5 - Depreciation Entry Details for "Listed Property"

well over 20,000 words. From an auditor's point of view, his focus is on—

(a) documentation that establishes the percentage of use in a qualified business,

(b) nature of the auditee's trade or business,

(c) whether used exclusively at the auditee's place of business, and

(d) the predominance of business use exceeding 50%.

For Schedule C businesses, this means the depreciation focus is on cars, trucks, boats, airplanes, computers, printers, copy machines, cellular phones, fax machines, photographic equipment, video cameras, and the like, and the leasing thereof. Luxury automobiles, desktop computers, and leased equipment are particularly scrutinized. In general, the maximum depreciation that can be taken on any automobile, luxury or otherwise, is about $15,000 . . . over a period of five years. Computers must also be depreciated over five years, and only if a clear and preponderant business use can be shown. Leased equipment is a bear trap, especially autos. Special "inclusion rules" apply. This means that the lessee . . . *must add an inclusion amount to his gross income* .

Perhaps the best way to acquaint you with the audit concerns of listed property is to present in edited form the detailed line entries expected of you on **Form 4562:** *Depreciation and Amortization*. Listed property is to be itemized in Part V of said form. Our rearrangement of Part V (Form 4562) is presented in Figure 9.5. We suggest that you read through this figure slowly, and digest the depth of detail required. You should also note that there is an entry distinction between more than, and less than, 50% business usage.

Depreciation Classes & Methods

If you have done your homework well and prepared for all of the above, chances are you will have "passed muster" to this point. There is just one more audit hurdle before you're home free. This hurdle pertains to the classification of property and the methods you used in figuring your overall depreciation deduction(s). These matters are often judgment calls. But whose judgment prevails: your judgment or that of the auditor? You have an interest in accelerating the depreciation; the auditor is unimpressed and wants to stretch things out. Stretching out materially reduces your depreciation deductions.

For many years, the IRS took a high-handed approach as to what constituted the "useful life" of a depreciable asset used in business. Its desire was to stretch out the useful lives of property to infinity. If property did not have an infinite life, then it had a "salvage value" at the end of its useful life. These adversarial tactics meant that any depreciation that the IRS allowed was absolutely minimized. This was the official position under the former rules of Section 167: Depreciation.

In the early 1980s, Section 168 was enacted. Section 168 essentially redefined the prior concept of depreciation; it became an *accelerated cost recovery* system. The term "accelerated" does away with the extended useful life concept and replaces it with specific (statutory) property classifications. The term "cost recovery" does away with the salvage value concept, and allows the business owner to recover every dollar of his cost in the property being depreciated.

RECOVERY CLASS	CLASS LIFESPAN	EXAMPLES
3 year	4 yrs or less	Power tools, dies, jigs, R&D items, computer software, carts & trays
5 year	4 to 10 yrs	Autos, light trucks, computers; equipment: office, shop, medical
7 year	10 to 16 yrs	Furniture, fixtures , & furnishings; heavy duty trucks, machinery, equip.
10 year	16 to 20 yrs	Boats, airplanes, hangars, storage sheds, barns, horticultural structures
15 year	20 to 25 yrs	Water, power, & communication systems; fruit bearing trees & vines
20 year	25 yrs or more	Municipal sewers, recycling plants, warehouses, bridges

Fig. 9.6 - Classification of Property for Cost Recovery Purposes

Section 168(e): *Classification of Property* statutorily groups all depreciable assets into those specific-year categories that we present in Figure 9.6. As you can surmise, other than buildings and structures on land, most Schedule C filers need deal with only 3-, 5-, 7-, and 10-year property classes. Of particular note, autos and computers are 5-year property. Up through 1986 they were 3-year property.

Various subsections in Section 168: *Accelerated Cost Recovery System* establish such "conventions" as mid-month, mid-quarter, and mid-year for the recovery starting point when property is placed in service. The recognized recovery methods may be: (a) 200% declining balance, (b) 150% declining balance, (c) straight line, (d) units-of-production, or (e) statutory percentages. Straight-line recovery is the reference base against which the other methods are measured for the amount of excess (or accelerated) depreciation taken. All "excess" is subject to recapture (under special rules).

We caution you against overusing any of the acceleration methods (a), (b), (d), or (e) above. Unless you can establish convincingly that the property item under audit is absolutely, positively, and exclusively used 100% for business — and this is where the auditor will test you — we suggest the middle course: straight line. If you properly classify your cost recovery property, and use straight line depreciation across-the-board, you'll find that auditors tend to be less picky. It is the *excess* depreciation that they want to whittle down.

Should the audit year be one in which the business use drops to 50% or below, all prior excess depreciation taken on that property will be recaptured. The presumption is that all prior non-audit-year business use also was below 50%. As mentioned when discussing the Section 179 election, any recapture of excess depreciation is an audit addition to your gross income on Schedule C.

10

SCHEDULE E ITEMS

> **Owners Of Rental/Royalty Property Report Income And Claim Expenses On Schedule E (Part I). The Principal Properties Involved Are Rental Dwelling Units, Nonresidential Real Estate, And Mineral Deposits (Including Timber Stands) On Natural Resource Land. Income From Business-Use Payers Is Verified By 1099s And From Others By Monthly Ledgers, Tenant/Lessee Contracts, And "For Rent" Ads And Listings. Most Expenses — Including Depreciation And Depletion — Are Allowed, But Not Capital Improvements. A Special $25,000 Net Loss Offset Is Allowed For 1040 Filers Under $100,000 AGI.**

Schedule E (Form 1040) is titled: **Supplemental Income and Loss.** It is a catchall for reporting passive income from rentals, royalties, farmland rentals, partnerships, S corporations, estates, trusts, and mortgage investment conduits. It consists of two pages, and is organized into five parts, namely:

Part I   —   Rentals and Royalties
Part II   —   Partnerships and S Corporations
Part III   —   Estates and Trusts
Part IV —   Mortgage Investment Conduits
Part V   —   Summary: Including Farm Rentals

In this chapter, we will not be concerned with Parts II through IV of Schedule E. The reason for bypassing these parts is that they involve "entities" in which the taxpayer/auditee is not the principal owner and manager. That is, the income and expenses are not under the direct supervision and control of the Form 1040 auditee. Professional managers are in control.

Audits involving partnerships, S corporations, estates, trusts, and mortgage investment conduits are conducted at the *entity level*. The audit results — whatever they may be — are "passed through" proportionately to each individual participant (who is a passive investor). Therefore, it would serve no constructive purpose here to discuss the entity audits of Parts II through IV. [Incidentally, an "S corporation" is a small business corporation with 75 or fewer shareholders; a "mortgage investment conduit" is an investment trust whose holdings consist primarily of real estate mortgages and foreclosure properties.]

Part I (Schedule E), on the other hand, consists of rental income property and royalty income property where the auditee is the outright owner of said property. In some cases, he may co-own the property with no more than three to five other persons. Each co-owner is a direct owner in the sense that he files his own Schedule E, itemizing his proportionate share of all income and all expenses. There are some 20,000,000 (20 million) Schedule E Part I filers each year. There are some "tax shelter" benefits to Schedule E filings, and it is for this reason that Schedules E are a common target for audit.

Rental & Royalty Properties

Rental property and royalty property are two distinct activities. The common thread between them is that there is ownership of property — real and/or tangible — which derives income. In tax terminology, it is property held for the "production or collection of income." In other words, the property itself produces the income. Any personal services therewith are minimal; they are not the predominant income factor. It is for this reason that Section 212: *Expenses for Production of Income*, allows certain expenses to be deducted in connection with said income.

Rental income property involves the rental or leasing of residential real estate, nonresidential real estate (commercial, industrial, farming), and tangible property such as vehicles (autos, boats, airplanes), machinery, and equipment. Royalty income property involves the leasing or licensing of rights to exploit the natural resources and mineral deposits of land, or the distribution and sale of creative works (such as books, patents, copyrights, film, works of art, etc.). All forms of income producing property are tax-treated much the same. However, in order to limit our discussion, we will give attention only to residential dwelling units and to natural resource property. These are the activities which produce the more significant income and expenses (for audit purposes).

We should comment a tad further on the distinction between rental income and royalty income. Whereas rent is measured by some unit of *time*, royalty is measured by some unit of *production*. For example, rent is X-dollars per month (or other period of time); royalty is Y-dollars per ton (or other unit of production). Rent involves the general use of property by a tenant, whereby the property owner does not participate in the income of the tenant. Royalty, on the other hand, involves the specific use of property by a lessee, whereby the property owner does participate in the income of the lessee. Consequently, rental income tends to be uniform throughout the year, whereas royalties tend to fluctuate. Understanding this distinction may help you to better respond to an uninformed auditor.

Personal Use Aspects

As we saw in the previous chapter, every auditor wants to explore the personal use aspects of any item for which a tax deduction is claimed. In the case of Schedule E (Part I), the almost exclusive focus is on residential dwelling units. Although natural resource property (such as timber land) and mineral exploration property (such as gold mining) have some conceivable personal use aspects, there is no statutory threshold of personal use as in the case of dwelling units.

A *dwelling unit* is a home, apartment, condominium, mobile home, boat, mini-motorhome, and the like. It is a place where a person or persons eat, sleep, bathe, entertain, and carry on everyday living. As such, a dwelling unit can be rented out for income purposes, but it also can be used as a residence by the owner, members of his family, and close friends.

The personal use of a dwelling is measured in *days*. Any part of a day is counted as a full day. A 24-hour "hotel day" is **not** the measure. One hour of personal use on a calendar day is a personal-use day. This is so stated in Section 280A(d)(2) as—

For the purpose of this section [disallowance of certain expenses], *the taxpayer shall be deemed to have used a dwelling for personal purposes for a day if, **for any part of such day**, the unit is used.* [Emphasis added.]

The term "personal use" includes:

(1) any use by the owner for personal purposes.
(2) use by any other person for personal purposes, if that person owns part of the unit.
(3) any use by a family member of the owner or co-owner (unless rented on a daily basis at fair rental value).
(4) any swapping arrangement with owners and co-owners of other dwelling units.
(5) use by anyone who pays less than fair rental value.

The statutory threshold for triggering the personal use rules is Section 280A(d)(1): *Use as Residence.* The language of this section is rather awkward to quote in part, without citing the entire 2,300-word statute. The essence is that if an auditee uses a rental dwelling unit more than 14 days of the full calendar year, OR more than 10 percent of the total days rented at fair value (for the year), stringent "allocable expense" rules trip into play.

So important is this personal-use threshold that the head portion of Schedule E (Part I) asks you specifically for a "Yes" or "No" answer. See Figure 10.1 for the head portion we're discussing.

If you answer "Yes," then you have to allocate all expenses (except property taxes and mortgage interest) in direct proportion to the number of fair rental days for the 365-day year.

If you answer "No," and the reported rental income appears eyeball small for the ownership year, the auditor will quiz you rather endlessly. For your defense, you need a third-party document stating your property's fair rental value. If the property is unrented at any time, you also need some supporting evidence that it was at all times available for rent, and was so offered to the general public.

"Active Participation" Defined

Because of the tax sheltering benefits of rental/royalty property, net losses are generally realized, such that these losses can be used to offset other sources of positive income. To restrict the use of shelter losses against other income, passive activity loss limitation

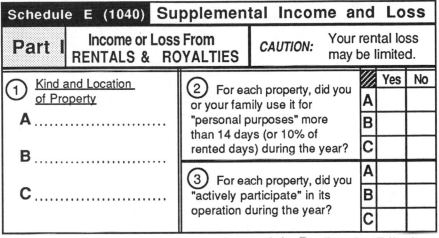

Fig. 10.1 - The Head Portion of Schedule E , Part I (Edited)

rules were enacted. This was done for the very first time in 1986. The embodiment is Section 469: *Passive Activity Losses . . . Limited*. The term "passive activity" includes *any* rental activity. In essence, the losses are limited to the passive income generated. Any excess loss is carried over to the next taxable year.

For rental real estate property, there is one exception to the general loss limit rule. This is the "active participation" rule of subsection 469(i)(6)(A). This subsection reads in full as—

> *An individual shall not be treated as actively participating with respect to any interest in any rental real estate activity for any period if, at any time during such period, such interest (including any interest of the spouse of the individual) is less than 10 percent (by value) of all interests in such activity.*

Establishing 10% participation (by value) in a rental activity is difficult to gauge . . . and probably difficult to enforce. As official guidance in this regard, the instructions to Schedule E (Part I) say:

> *The active participation requirement can be met without regular, continuous, and substantial involvement in operations. But you must have participated in making management decisions or arranging for others to provide services (such as repairs), in a significant and bona fide sense. Management decisions that are*

relevant in this context include approving new tenants, deciding on rental terms, approving capital or repair expenditures, and other similar decisions.

As you can see in Figure 10.1, the question of active participation is directed to you in "Yes" or "No" fashion. If "Yes," you may be able to use up to $25,000 in net losses for the audit year. We'll tell you more about this below.

Your Deductible Expenses

Rather than telling what deductions are allowable against your rental/royalty incomes, we present a listing of the deductions in Figure 10.2. As you glance down the list, most of them are what you would expect when managing income-producing property of any form. Note that, at item 14, there is space for adding other directly-related and necessary expenses, such as deposit refunds, gardening, pool service, pest control, cleaning services, and so on.

Particularly note item 7: Mortgage interest (in Figure 10.2). This is mortgage-type interest that you pay to financial institutions only. This is similar to the mortgage payments discussed in Chapter 8 with respect to Schedule A. All mortgage interest to financial institutions is computer matched . . . a la Figure 8.3. The point here is that you had better have the lender-prepared Forms 1098 to back up your entries at item 7. If you have co-owners (other than your spouse), you have a matching problem. Get clarifying statements from your co-owners, and other pertinent documents (such as title deeds and mortgage contracts) showing your share of ownership of each property.

If you paid any kind of maintenance fees, management fees, commissions, or legal and accounting fees in excess of $600 to each payee, you need supporting 1099-MISCs. Recall Figure 9.3. If you pay wages or salaries, you'll need supporting W-2s.

There are two catchall type items that an auditor will definitely check on. These are *repairs* (item 9 in Figure 10.2) and *supplies* (item 10). What the auditor is looking for is: Have you engaged in extensive remodeling and renovation that properly should be classed as an "improvement" rather than repairs and supplies? The cost of improvements is depreciable — stretched out — whereas repairs and supplies are currently expensed. Improvements are such matters as a new roof, complete painting (inside or outside), remodeling kitchen (or bath), conversion to multiple dwelling units,

Sch.E	Part I	Income or Loss from Rentals & Royalties			
INCOME		**Properties**			**TOTALS**
		A	**B**	**C**	
EXPENSES					
1	Advertising				
2	Auto & travel				
3	Cleaning & maint.				
4	Commissions				
5	Insurance				
6	Legal & accounting				
7	Mortgage interest				
8	Other interest				
9	Repairs				
10	Supplies				
11	Taxes				
12	Utilities				
13	Wages & salaries				
14	....	....	....	....	*Other Expenses. List Carefully.*
	Subtotal Expenses				
15	Depreciation or depletion $*$				
	Total Expenses				
	NET INCOME OR (LOSS)				
$*$ See Instructions		Caution : See Loss Limitations Form 8582			

Fig. 10.2 - The Preprinted Deduction Lines on Schedule E , Part I

relandscaping, new fence and driveway, and extensive renovations and building code updates to property that has been in existence 50 years or more.

Overall, your best audit bet is to package every entry item of expenses on your Schedule E, separately and sequentially, property by property. Attach all invoices and cancelled checks (or other receipts for payment). If you have total expenses that exceed your total income, property by property, you know the auditor is going to pick away at you. So, go loaded for bear.

Documentation of Income

If your expenses exceed your income on a property-by-property basis, you'll be asked to document the income separately for each property reported on Schedule E. If your income exceeds your expenses, chances are your expenses will not be examined too closely. The audit presumption is that most auditees participate in rental/royalty property for the tax benefits (loss writeoffs) rather than for additional taxable income.

Consequently, income documentation becomes important for net loss situations, property by property.

What kind of rental/royalty income documentation should you have?

If the property is rented or leased to a person or entity using the property for business purposes, chances are that person or entity would have forwarded to you a 1099-MISC for the rents/royalties paid. That business-use person or entity will be taking the payments to you on his/its own tax return. Box 1 of Form 1099-MISC (in Figure 7.3) is for "rents," whereas Box 2 is for "royalties."

Otherwise, the only income documentation that you have — or should have — is a *rents/royalties income ledger*. When you answer "Yes" to the active participation question (in Figure 10.1), you are expected to act like a manager and keep a running monthly account of each income payment that you receive. Also, you should have entered into a written rental agreement with each dwelling unit tenant, and/or a royalty agreement with each natural resource lessee. Make sure that these agreements (contracts) are updated and part of your Schedule E records at all times. During periods of vacancies and nonincome, you should have copies of your "for rent" ads and listings in public places.

If you receive security deposits or advance rents or royalties, be sure to note this fact in your income ledger. Keep a separate clearly identified column for this purpose. If you refund any deposit or advance, said refunds become a deductible expense.

The gist of the type of rental/royalty income documentation that will stand you in good stead for audit is depicted in Figure 10.3. If this is your first Schedule E audit, you should pursue the documentation of Figure 10.3 religiously. You want to convince the auditor that you are renting at competitive rates, and that you are trying to get the best income that you can.

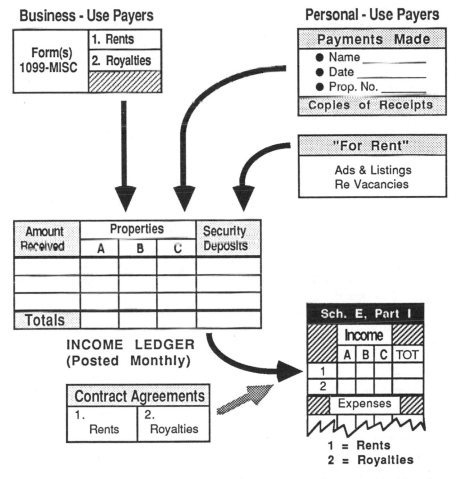

Fig. 10.3 - Documentation for Rental/Royalty Income Verification

Depreciation: Straight Line

As with any business-use property, you are allowed a depreciation deduction for the "wear, tear, and obsolescence" therewith. In the case of a dwelling unit, you are allowed depreciation for the structures, attachments to structures, and improvements to structures. You are allowed **no depreciation for land**. However, you are allowed separated depreciation for furniture, fixtures, furnishings, and appliances within, or associated with, the dwelling structures.

For the structural portion of rental real property acquired after 1986, the depreciation method **must be** straight line. If residential realty, the cost recovery life is 27.5 years. If nonresidential realty, the cost recovery life is 31.5 years (before May 13, 1993); otherwise, 39 years. You have no choice. These recovery lives and method are fixed by tax code Sections 168(b)(3)(A), (B), and 168(c)(1).

Furthermore, you must use the "mid-month" convention. This means that if you acquired the property on or before the 14th of the month, you get a full month's depreciation for the acquisition month. If you cease renting or dispose of the property on or before the 14th day of the month, you get no depreciation for the disposition month.

When you acquire or dispose of rental real estate, unavoidably there is land associated with it. Since the land is part of the acquisition or disposition package, how do you separate it out? This is where your *property tax statement* (from the county assessor's office) comes in handy.

Most official statements for assessed property tax display, separately, a value for land and a value for improvements. The valuations themselves may not — and often are not — true market values. Yet, the *relative* values shown are IRS-accepted as reasonably proper, since they are prepared by a "third party." Consequently, it is a matter of using the assessor's values for determining the structural (fractional) part of your property without the associated land.

Your building structure fraction is simply—

$$\text{Structure} = \frac{\text{Improvements}}{\text{Land} + \text{Improvements}} = \underline{\hspace{1cm}}\%$$

You multiply your rental realty acquisition cost by this structure fraction to establish the initial cost basis for depreciating the structural portion of each of your rental realties. Your property tax statement and your acquisition settlement statement are the two audit documents you need for verifying your initial depreciation basis.

As to that tangible personal property associated with your rental dwelling units, you can use the appropriate recovery lives from Figure 9.6 (on page 9-23).

Depletion of Natural Resources

If you show royalty income from natural resource property on your Schedule E, you are allowed a *depletion* deduction. Depletion is the exhaustion of a nonreplenishable resource such as oil and gas, geothermal deposits, iron and copper ores, asbestos and sulphur, aluminum and coal, clay and stone, standing timber, and a host of other minerals and nonminerals. There are two kinds of depletion allowances, namely: cost depletion (Section 612) and percentage depletion (Section 613).

Cost depletion uses the concept of determinable total units of extraction of the natural deposit. One's cost depletion is that fraction of the total deposit which is extracted/removed during each taxable year. Thus, the fraction may change from year to year. The depletion fraction is applicable only to the acquisition cost of the actual deposit itself. It is *not* applicable to the land which houses or contains the deposit. Consequently, one's cost basis in the deposit must be clearly distinguishable from the cost of the land containing it. Herein lies the key to endless audit issues involving cost depletion.

Percentage depletion, on the other hand, is simpler in concept, but is more complex in regulatory detail. Percentage depletion allows a statutory fixed percentage of the gross annual income from sale of the deposit to be deducted. The statutory percentages are prescribed in Sections 613(b) and 613A. These percentages range from 22% down to 5%, depending on the type of resource being extracted. The percentages apply to the gross royalties from the property.

The depletion deduction (cost or percentage) is allowed only to the owner of an *economic interest* in the depletable resource. An economic interest consists of the right to income from extraction of the resource, plus a capital investment in the resource(s) in place.

An economic interest is measured by *units of production/extraction* and not by the passage of time.

Regulation 1.611-1(b): ***Economic Interest***, is particularly pertinent here. Among its voluminous wordage, this regulation states that—

> *An economic interest is possessed in every case in which the taxpayer has acquired by investment any interest in mineral in place or standing timber and secures, by any form of legal relationship, income derived from the extraction of the mineral or severance of the timber, to which he must look for a return of his capital.*

In other words, an economic interest is ownership (or rights to ownership) of a natural resource, where part of the income from extraction of the resource is treated as return of capital. As one gets his capital investment back, his initial basis in the resource property is correspondingly reduced.

In an audit situation, each deposit of a depletable resource must be separately described. So, too, must the (horizontal) surface area of land containing each deposit be described. Thus, the land and its resource must be separately cost identified. If not, the auditor will assign everything to land . . . which is nondepletable.

The $25,000 "Loss Limit" Rule

In the case of rental real estate with active participation, there is a special $25,000 loss allowance that we said we would tell you about. The $25,000 amount is the maximum net losses from all realty activities that can be used to offset other sources of positive income on Form 1040. It is not an automatic allowance; there are certain conditions attached.

In the tax code, this allowance is titled: ***$25,000 Offset for Rental Real Estate Activities***. This is the embodiment of Section 469(i). In pertinent part, this section reads—

> *(1) In the case of any **natural person**, subsection (a)* [the general disallowance of all net passive activity losses] *shall not apply to that portion of the passive activity loss . . . which is attributable to **all** rental real estate activities with respect to which such individual actively participated in such taxable year.*

*(2) The **aggregate amount** to which paragraph (1) applies for any taxable year shall not exceed $25,000.* [Emphasis added.]

As emphasized above, only individual Form 1040 filers are eligible for the $25,000 offset allowance. It is not available to entities such as partnerships, estates, trusts, corporations, or others. Also, the $25,000 is the aggregate total allowable loss from all rental real estate; it is *not* a per property allowance.

Furthermore, the full $25,000 is only available to 1040 filers whose *modified* adjusted gross income (MAGI) is less than $100,000. It is not available to those whose MAGI exceeds $150,000 for the taxable year. Between MAGI's of $100,000 and $150,000, the $25,000 is "phased out" (Sec. 469(i)(3)).

One's modified AGI is his regular Form 1040 AGI without taking into account any passive activity losses, and without any deduction benefits for contributions to qualified retirement plans. One's MAGI is essentially his total positive income before the $25,000 loss allowance amount is computed. For every $2,000 of MAGI over $100,000, one loses $1,000 of the $25,000 offset.

Form 8582	Passive Activity Loss Limitations			Year	
Part II	Rental Real Estate With Active Participation				
1	Enter total pertinent losses from Schedule E		$		
2	Enter $150,000		*	$	
3	Enter modified AGI	but not less than zero	$		
4	Subtract 3 from 2	but not less than zero	$		
5	Multiply Line 4 by 50% :	Do not enter more than $25,000	*	$	
6	Enter the <u>SMALLER OF</u> Line 1 or Line 5 ➤		$		
Allocate Line 6 proportionately to each property in Line 1					
	* See instructions for married filing separately				

Fig. 10.4 - The Special Loss Allowance for Rental Real Estate

Determination of one's eligible portion of the $25,000 offset is made on Form 8582: Passive Activity Loss Limitations. In Part II, there is a special computational sequence which we have edited and presented in Figure 10.4. The primary purpose of the computation is to run through the phase-out aspects for MAGI's between $100,000 and $150,000. If your MAGI is below $100,000, you do not need Form 8582, insofar as your rental real estate activities are concerned.

Exception for R.E. Professionals

Commencing in 1994, an exception to the $25,000 offset limit was enacted to apply to real estate professionals. This is subsection 469(c)(7): *Special Rules for Taxpayers in Real Property Business*. The substantive requirement is that—

*more than one-half of personal services . . . [be] performed in real property trades or businesses in which the taxpayer materially participates, **and** such taxpayer performs more than 750 hours of services during the taxable year.* [Emphasis added.]

The term "real property trade or business" means—

any real property development, redevelopment, acquisition, conversion, rental, operation, management, leasing, or brokerage trade or business.

If you qualify as an R.E. professional, you signify this in Part V (Summary) of Schedule E at the line which reads—

Reconciliation for Real Estate Professionals . . . enter the net income or (loss) you reported anywhere on Form 1040 from all rental real estate activities in which you materially participated. $_____

Obviously, if you have significant losses in your material participation (personal service) business(es), and you have these losses two or three years in a row, the auditor is going to question you — and requestion you — about your lifestyle. His/her natural cynicism is: If you are truly a "professional," you should be earning a livelihood in at least some segment of the real property industry.

11

PRICKLY ISSUES

Audits Sometimes Involve Peripheral Issues On Which The IRS Takes A Stance Beyond Ordinary Reasoning. Auditors May Transgress Published Regulations Regarding "Adequate Records," "Inclusion Amounts," "Focal-Point" Matters, Not-For-Profit Activities, And "At Risk" Limitations. If You Claim Business Use Of A "Luxury" Auto, Any Travel Or Entertainment, Office-At-Home, Or Alimony Paid, You Are In For A Difficult Time. Alimony (Spousal Support) Must Be Distinctly Separated From Child Support And Property Settlement Payments. Multiple "Add-Backs" For Alternate Minimum Tax (AMT) May Apply.

A "prickly issue" is ordinarily, but not necessarily, an issue of major importance in the administration of tax law. Its importance may rest on the fact that it tests a certain section of the Internal Revenue Code, or that it could establish a pattern for a large number of taxpayers similarly situated. The premise is that if the issue is allowed to go unchallenged in each and every instance, there could develop a major shortage in federal revenues.

The amount of a prickly issue on one individual's tax return in and of itself may not be significant. It could be as little as $100, for example. But if, say, 30 million taxpayers took advantage of the item, the sum of *3 billion* dollars ($3,000,000,000) would be at stake. In this kind of situation, the IRS can become paranoid.

Sometimes, what is not inherently an audit issue is asserted as such. This is so that the IRS can build up more rules and regulations for itself to administer. It does this by challenging Congress to enact new tax laws where none currently exist. It can pick a relatively small matter, examine it out of proportion to reality, build up a backlog of cases on it, then go to Congress and demand more tax legislation.

An auditee never knows when he is confronting a prickly issue. The outward appearances are the same as any other "routine" audit matter. The only clue that one gets is that the procedures begin to transgress ordinary human reasoning. When an auditor starts to lock his/her nose up high and hard, and refuses reason, you know that you have invaded prime issue territory. You can still win, but only if you have covered your tax trail perfectly. You have to meet *every letter* of the law: not just its general intent.

Business Mileage Log

We skipped over this matter previously, but we now want to stress its importance. It is an issue which affects every audit in which so much as 100 miles of business usage of an auto is claimed. The prickly item? A business *mileage log*. So simple in concept, yet so few auditees are prepared with it.

For the auditor, it's almost like a teaser question: "Do you have a mileage log?" You can sense that he or she is waiting with baited breath for your answer.

Nowhere in the tax code does it specifically use the phrase "mileage log" with respect to business use of an auto. The nearest to this is Section 274(d)(4), to wit—

> *No deduction . . . shall be allowed . . . with respect to any listed property* [passenger automobile] *. . . unless the taxpayer substantiates by **adequate records** or by sufficient evidence corroborating the taxpayer's own statement.* [Emphasis added.]

Then Regulation 1.274-5(c)(2) amplifies this by saying, in part, that—

> *(i) To meet the "adequate records" requirements of section 274(d), a taxpayer **shall maintain** an account book, diary, statement of expense or similar record.*
> *(ii) An account book, diary . . . or similar record must be prepared or maintained in such manner that each recording of an*

element of expenditure is made **at or near** *the time of the expenditure.* [Emphasis added.]

Thus, if you claim any business use of passenger auto whatsoever, you . . . *shall maintain* . . . "an account book, diary, or similar record" of your business mileage.

A mileage log should show the business destination, purpose, and mileage for each day of claimed business use. You need a 365-day record book for this. In the first page of the book you show the odometer reading at the beginning of the year, and at the end of the year. If you make certain repeated business trips, you can code each destination on a separate page with its round trip mileage. Then diary the code numbers only. If you work a regular route or territory, a road map with the business destinations highlighted thereon can be inserted into the diary. Also helpful are repair and maintenance invoices. These invoices usually show third-party entries of your odometer readings. An auditor uses these readings to help cross-check your total business mileage for the year.

Even if you make copious notes on scraps of paper and backs of envelopes during the year, we urge that you purchase a preprinted and dated pocket-size business diary. For each year, make the clean entries whenever it is most convenient for you.

So when an auditor asks you: "Where's your mileage log?", reach in your pocket and hand it to him. Then sit back and enjoy the surprised look on the auditor's face.

Leasing Luxury Autos

Would you believe that the IRS defines a "luxury auto" as costing more than $15,000? Yes, it really does. (Wonder how many IRS officials limit their auto purchases to less than $15,000?)

The cost definition of a luxury auto is not spelled out in the tax code. There is mention of "luxury automobiles" in Section 280F(a): *Limitation on Amount of . . . Depreciation for Luxury Automobiles.* One has to construct the cost by adding up to five years of limited depreciation, and applying an inflation factor (commencing 1990). As of 1996, the five years of limited depreciation were: $3,060 (1st yr); $4,900 (2nd yr); $2,950 (3rd yr); $1,775 (4th yr); and $1,775 (5th yr). These depreciations add up to $14,460. Add $400 for each year's inflation, and you come up with $14,860 for 1997.

When you look at the above depreciation amounts each year, as a potential expense deduction, you probably can't get very excited. Therefore, it is tempting not to buy an auto for business purposes, but to lease one instead. You would do this with the idea of writing off your annual lease payments as a prorata business expense.

Hold it!

Before you dash out to lease an auto for business purposes, you should be aware of the new income inclusion rules. That is, an *inclusion amount* is **added to** your gross income for each year or part year of your lease. Surprised?

Regulation 1.280F-7(a)(1) says, in part—

If a taxpayer leases a passenger automobile after December 31, 1986, the taxpayer must include in gross income an inclusion amount determined [from IRS tables] *for each taxable year during which the taxpayer leases the automobile.*

The parenthetically referenced IRS tables are officially designated: **Leased Business Auto Inclusion Table**, depending on the year you start the lease. Each table covers a five-year leasing period. For each full lease year, the tables show an inclusion dollar amount corresponding to various fair market values of the leased vehicle. The tables start at about $15,000 and go to $250,000 (including all accessories).

Suppose, for example, that you leased a vehicle with tape deck, air conditioning, and cellular phone total valued at $50,000. (This would be $35,000 of "luxuriating.") From Table 8 (1997), in the third year of your lease, you would add $925 to your gross income. For the five-year lease period, you would include a total of $4,225 to your gross income. (The inclusion amounts increase with each succeeding lease year.)

At time of audit, the examiner would want to see your auto leasing agreement. If you did not show an inclusion amount for each year that you claimed business auto expenses, he would add the cumulative inclusion amount to your gross income for the audit year. To prevent this cumulative impact, get hold of your applicable-year IRS leased-auto inclusion table now.

Travel & Entertainment

One issue that's guaranteed to be a "hot button" audit item is travel and entertainment expenses. Taxpayers claiming these expenses repeatedly are often highly personable persons. As such, they usually lack the necessary self-discipline for good record-keeping. If audited, they rely on personality rather than on perseverance. They are an easy prey for auditors who need to maintain or enhance their quota performance for additional tax revenues.

The term "travel and entertainment" (T & E) is a collective phrase, not limited to travel and entertainment only. It covers a broad range of business-associated deductions where there is likelihood of personal enjoyment under the guise of a business purpose.

Included under T & E expenses are such items as use of auto, taxis, air travel, boat, bus, limousine, and so on. Also included are meals (lunches), lodging, laundry, tips, telephone, small gifts (booze, flowers, candy), event fees, small tools, supplies, educational courses, and other out-of-pocket expenses associated with carrying on one's trade, business, profession, or occupation. Except for airfares and lodging away from home, vouchers, receipts, or other documentation are seldom issued by payees in the ordinary course of business. Consequently, if you are a T & E auditee, you'll have to display superb recordkeeping know-how. In Figure 11.1, we outline the audit expectations of you.

There is nothing illegal about claiming T & E expenses, so long as each is incurred "directly," and "in pursuit of" your business affairs, and is "ordinary and necessary" for the conduct thereof. Just be aware of Code Section 274: *Disallowance of Certain Entertainment, Etc. Expenses*, with its 40+ subsections. You can be sure that if an auditor can find some word or phrase in Section 274 to disallow an item of T & E, he/she will assert it. So, do your homework, build your case, and organize your expenses along the lines of Figure 11.1.

Office-at-Home

Anyone in a trade, business, or profession who uses a portion of his home as a regular place of business may deduct certain expenses in connection therewith. The deduction is available to Schedule A filers (employees and professionals), Schedule C filers (self-employed persons), Schedule E filers (owners of income property), and Schedule F filers (farming, fishing, ranching, etc.). The tax rules on point are rather stringent, but they are not totally

EXPENSE CATEGORY	INFORMATION REQUIRED	TYPE OF SUBSTANTIATION
TRAVEL: AWAY FROM HOME OVERNIGHT		
1. Air fare	Date, place, purpose	Ticket stubs
2. Boat or train	Date, place, purpose	Ticket stubs
3. Bus or taxi	Date & amount	Travel log
4. Car rental	Date, place, purpose	Rental contract
5. Meals & tips	Date, amount, which	Restaurant stubs
6. Lodging	Date, place, purpose	Lodging bill
7. Laundry & baggage	Date, amount, what	Travel log
8. Event fees	Business purpose	Ticket stubs
9. Tools & supplies	Description & purpose	Dated cash receipts
10. Phone & telex	Description & purpose	Travel log
TRANSPORTATION: WITHIN TAX HOME AREA		
1. Auto mileage	Where, when, why	Mileage log
2. Other transport	Where, when, why	Ticket stubs
3. Business lunches	Date, amount, who	Restaurant stubs
4. Treats & snacks	Date & amount	Expense log
5. Parking & tolls	Date & amount	Expense log
6. Public phone	Date, amount, who	Expense log
7. Tools & supplies	Description & purpose	Dated cash receipts
8. Courses & seminars	Business relationship	Tuition receipts
9. Books & journals	Subject & amount	Dated cash receipts
10. Uniforms & access.	Amount, why needed	Purchase slips
ENTERTAINMENT: AT A RECOGNIZED FACILITY		
1. Small gifts	Description, purpose	Dated cash receipts
2. Banquet meals	Date,amount,why,who	Certified receipts
3. Sporting events	Date,amount,why,who	Certified receipts
4. Social events	Date,amount,why,who	Certified receipts
5. Conventions, U.S.	Description & purpose	Programs & receipts
6. Conventions, foreign	How business related	Sponsorship records
7. Cruise ship	How business related	Certified workshops
8. Sight seeing trip	How business related	Certified attendance
9. Yacht outings	Date,what,where,why	Official log: time in/out
10. Pleasure flights	Date,what,where,why	Official log: time in/out

Fig. 11.1 - How T&E Expenses Should Be Itemized

unreasonable. It is the IRS's interpretation that transgresses the bounds of ordinary reason.

The applicable tax law is Section 280A(a): *Disallowance of Certain Expenses in Connection with Business Use of Home, Etc.* The IRS interprets "certain" expenses to mean all expenses and therefore total disallowance.

The IRS tries to ignore the statutory exceptions to the general disallowance rule. The exceptions are identified in subsection 280A(c): *Exceptions for Certain Business Use.* This subsection reads in pertinent part—

> *Subsection (a) shall not apply to any item to the extent such item is allocable to a portion of the dwelling unit which is exclusively used on a regular basis—*
> *(A) as the principal place of business for any trade or business of the taxpayer,*
> *(B) as a place of business which is used by patients, clients, or customers in meeting or dealing with the taxpayer in the normal course of his trade or business, or*
> *(C) in the case of a separate structure which is not attached to the dwelling unit, in connection with the taxpayer's trade or business. [Emphasis added.]*

Of the options (A), (B), or (C) above, the most controversial is the "principal place" test. In *N.E. Soliman* [SCT, 93-1 USTC ¶ 50,014], the Supreme Court interpreted the word "principal" to mean *the most important, consequential, or influential* place where business is conducted. This includes such factors as:

(1) the relative importance of the activities performed at each business location (if more than one location is involved),
(2) the time spent at each location, and
(3) the point at which goods and services are delivered.

The essence of the High Court view was that one's principal place of business had to be the location at which the dominant portion of one's work is performed. Congress in 1997, however, adopted a different view. It amended the wording of Subsection 280A(c)(1) to include *administrative or management activities*, if no other suitable location were used. So important is the "principal place" issue that we depict its essential elements in Figure 11.2.

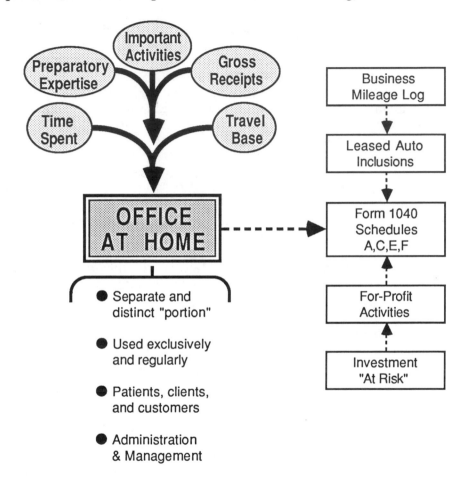

Fig. 11.2 - "Principal Place" Aspects of One's Office-at-Home

What about multiple businesses by the same taxpayer? Suppose a taxpayer had two distinctly separate trades or businesses. Could he have two offices-at-home?

You know what the IRS position would be. It says "No." It says all businesses by the same taxpayer must be conducted from the same office-at-home. The tax law says: "for *any* trade or business." It doesn't say "all" trades or businesses. The point that we are trying to get across here is that the IRS often abuses the law, rather than pursuing its reasonable interpretation as intended by Congress.

Not-for-Profit Activities

Another area where the IRS often abuses its discretion is the not-for-profit presumption of Section 183. Subsection (a) is the general rule which says that—

If such activity is not engaged in for profit, no deduction attributable to such activity shall be allowed.

In contrast, subsection (d): **Presumption**, goes on to say—

*If the gross income derived from an activity for 3 or more of the taxable years in the period of 5 consecutive taxable years which ends with the taxable year exceeds the deductions attributable to such activity, . . . then, . . . such activity **shall be presumed** . . . for such taxable year to be an activity engaged in for profit.* [Emphasis added.]

Section 183(d) is a presumption of law; it is not a mandate of law. The presumption is that if you make a profit in three out of five consecutive years, you are profit motivated. If you do not make a profit in three out of five years, you are not profit motivated. You're a flake engaged in some sort of hobby for personal pleasure.

Section 183(d) is a crutch that the IRS and its auditors use to disallow any deduction or net loss from an activity which is new, entrepreneurial, or risk-taking. They use it to deny any expenditure which they don't understand. The trial and errors, and tribulations, of entrepreneurship are truly beyond their comprehension. Sometimes it takes 10 to 15 years before entrepreneurship blossoms into a successful business.

The possibility of profit over a longer period of time than five years appears to be taken into account by Regulation 1.183-2(a). It uses the "objective standards" approach to interpreting Section 183. In relevant part, this regulation says—

*Although a reasonable expectation of profit is not required, the facts and circumstances must indicate that the taxpayer **entered*** *into the activity, or continued the activity with the objective of making a profit. In determining whether such an objective exists, it may be sufficient that there is a small chance of making a large profit.* [Emphasis added.]

In other words, it is one's bona fide intent that counts, rather than whether his "bottom line" is positive or negative for the activity at issue.

To assess this intent, Regulation 1.183-2(b) lists the relevant factors that IRS auditors are supposed to use. In highly abbreviated form, this regulation states that—

Among the factors which should normally be taken into account are the following:
(1) Manner in which the taxpayer carries on the activity.
(2) The expertise of the taxpayer or his advisors.
(3) The time and effort expended by the taxpayer in carrying on the activity.
(4) Expectation that the assets used in activity may appreciate in value.
(5) The success of the taxpayer in carrying on other similar or dissimilar activities.
(6) The taxpayer's history of income or losses with respect to the activity.
(7) The amount of occasional profits, if any, which are earned.
(8) The financial status of the taxpayer.
(9) Elements of personal pleasure or recreation.

The problem with regulations such as the above is that many IRS auditors do not read them. If and when they do, they pick on one or two items to use against you, and ignore those in your favor. If push comes to shove, an auditor can always say "No." You then have to prove him (or her) wrong.

"At Risk" Limitation Rule

As if it were not enough that the IRS has audit authority to say "No," based on whim and conjecture, it also has authority to determine how much money is "at risk" in designated activities. The purpose is to limit the amount of loss writeoff that can be taken in a given taxable year. The yardstick is not profit or loss in the ordinary sense, but how much personal-risk money one has on the line. Targeted are those enterprises motivated more by tax benefits than by true economic gain: tax shelters, in other words.

The particular law on point is Section 465: *Deductions Limited to Amount at Risk*. Subsection (a), the general rule, says—

> *In the case of an individual* [or personal holding company] . . . *engaged in an activity to which this section applies, any loss from such activity for the taxable year shall be allowed only to the extent of the aggregate amount with which the taxpayer is at risk . . . for such activity at the close of the taxable year.* [Emphasis added.]

As per subsection (c), this loss limit rule applies specifically to the following activities:

(1) Holding, producing, or distributing motion picture films or video tapes.
(2) Farming, including any agricultural commodity, fruit and nut trees, animal breeding, and cattle raising.
(3) Equipment leasing such as computers, cargo containers, telecommunications, etc.
(4) Exploring for, or exploiting, oil and gas resources.
(5) Exploring for, or exploiting, geothermal deposits.
(6) Any other activity (which is not above) of carrying on a trade or business or for the production of income.

In other words, anything venturesome that's not tried and true. Full risk capital must be on the line.

Category (6) — the catchall group — is intended to include all Schedule C filers, all Schedule E filers, and all Schedule F filers (the "F" is for farming). At the bottom line of each of these schedules, there is a preprinted directive:

> *If you have a loss, you MUST check the box that describes your investment in this activity:*
> ☐ *All investment is at risk*
> ☐ *Some investment is at risk*

If, as an auditee, any of your Schedules C, E, or F show a loss and you missed checking one of the two boxes, the auditor has authority to delete the amount of loss and reset the bottom line to zero. In tax administration terminology, this is called: non-recognition of loss.

If you checked "All at risk," the auditor may question you, and have you produce documentation of—

(a) the amount of after-tax money you contributed to the activity,
(b) the adjusted basis of any property you contributed,
(c) any borrowed money to the extent that you are personally liable for repayment, and/or
(d) the professionally appraised value of any pledged property (for securing a loan) to the extent of your ownership therein.

If you checked "Some at risk," the auditor will ask you for **Form 6198**: At-Risk Limitations. This is a very complex form. When you start reading its 8,000+ words of instructions, you'll go back and check the "All at risk" box. If your amount at risk is greater than your loss, the loss can be recognized.

Alimony Paid & Received

As we all know, divorce is common these days. There is disruption of marriage whereby two persons, formerly filing one joint return, file two returns separately. For a time at least, there is transfer of money from one spouse (or former spouse) to the other spouse (or former spouse). The one making the payments is the *payer* spouse; the one receiving the payments is the *payee* spouse. In this situation, divorce often becomes a lucrative source of additional revenue to the IRS.

In an incident-to-divorce situation, there are, generally, three kinds of "transfer payments." If children are involved, there are child support payments. Child support is not deductible by the payer, nor includible by the payee. If property is involved, there are property-equalizing payments. These are not deductible, nor includible. And, thirdly, there are support payments to the lesser employed spouse or former spouse. If the support payments commence before the divorce is final, they are called "separate maintenance." If made after the divorce is final, they are called "alimony."

The first auditee in a divorce situation is the payer spouse. If the payments are clearly distinguishable as alimony (or separate maintenance), the payer spouse gets a deduction (adjustment to income). The payee spouse gets an inclusion (addition) to income. This sounds simple enough. The problem is that the payments are seldom clearly distinguishable as alimony; they are usually mixed together with child support and property settlement. How many divorce attorneys do you know who write clearly distinguishable alimony clauses in a decree?

The subject of alimony and separate maintenance payments is addressed in Sections 215 and 71 of the tax code. The gist of Section 215(a) and (b) is —

*In the case of an individual, there shall be **allowed as a deduction** an amount equal to the alimony or separate maintenance payments paid during such individual's taxable year . . . **which is includible in** the gross income of the recipient.* [Emphasis added.]

The full wording of Section 71(a) is—

Gross income includes amounts received as alimony or separate maintenance payments.

The payee spouse has to provide his or her social security number to the payer spouse. The payer spouse, in turn, has to cross-reference the payee's number on the payer's tax return. [Sec. 215(c)(1),(2).] The net result is the computer-matching opportunity that we depict in Figure 11.3. Thus, the auditor has two (usually noncooperative) taxpayers on the opposite sides of the tax barrel.

If the amount of alimony is not clear or distinguishable, guess what happens?

Answer: The auditor simply disallows all payment deductions by the payer AND, simultaneously, *adds* all payments (including child support and property settlement) to the payee spouse's income. This is a clear "win-win" for the IRS.

Obviously, if your audit involves the issue of alimony, you and your former spouse had better get your tax acts together.

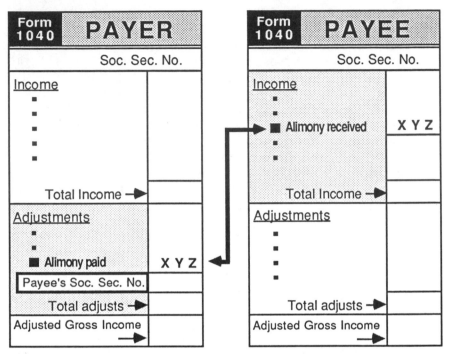

Fig. 11.3 - Computer-Matching Alimony Amounts on Forms 1040

Alternative Minimum Tax

There is just one other prickly issue that we should touch on, before wrapping up this chapter. It is the alternative minimum tax (AMT). The AMT is a separate and independent computational system of its own. It is an auditor's last chance to get you, even if you have satisfied all of his previous testings.

The AMT is a completely separate tax addressed in Sections 55 through 59 of the Internal Revenue Code. The "flavor" of these sections is put forth in subsection 55(a). This subsection reads—

> There is hereby imposed (**in addition to** any other tax imposed by this subtitle) a tax equal to **the excess** (if any) of—
> (1) the tentative minimum tax for the taxable year, over
> (2) **the regular tax** for the taxable year. [Emphasis added.]

The regular tax is that which appears on page 2 of Form 1040 at the entry next below the line titled: Taxable income. This is the tax regularly computed by using the tax rate schedules for single, head of household, married filing jointly, or married filing separately.

The sole purpose of AMT, as alleged, is to ensure that no taxpayer who has substantial economic income can avoid significant tax liability by using exclusions, deductions, and credits. In theory, AMT is based on *adding back* all — or most all — of the tax benefits previously taken properly. In reality, it is a punitive measure for successful tax planning and for successful audit substantiation.

As a simple add-back example, take the matter of your standard deduction (if used in lieu of itemized deductions). This is that entry line on your Form 1040 which you subtract before arriving at your "taxable income." Under AMT theory, your standard deduction (and most of your itemized deductions if used alternatively to the standard deduction) is whisked away from you. It is **added to** your regular taxable income for starting the AMT computation.

Altogether, there are approximately 30 add-backs influencing AMT. Approximately 20 are classed as "adjustments"; the other 10 are classed as "tax preferences." For instructional simplicity, we list these add-backs, in edited form, in Figure 11.4. Officially, they are listed on **Form 6251**: *Alternative Minimum Tax—Individuals*. If any of the add-backs relate to you, you are urged to obtain Form 6251 and its 8,500-word set of instructions. Obviously, you do this before going to audit.

The auditor, of course, is interested in packing onto Form 6251 all add-backs that he possibly can. His goal is to pump up your *alternative minimum taxable income* (AMTI).

From the auditor's AMTI amount, you are entitled to those specific exemptions set forth in Section 55(d). In abbreviated and edited form, the statutory exemption amounts are:

1. For married filing separately—
   ☐ $22,500 less 25% of AMTI in excess of $75,000

2. For singles and heads of household—
   ☐ $33,750 less 25% of AMTI in excess of $112,500

3. For married filing jointly—
   ☐ $45,000 less 25% of AMTI in excess of $150,000

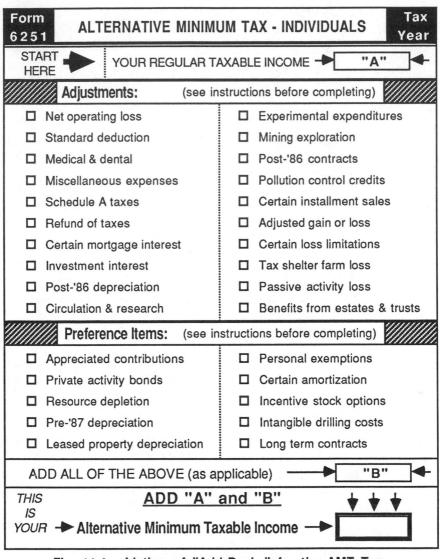

Fig. 11.4 - Listing of "Add-Backs" for the AMT Tax

After the applicable exemption amount, the AMT 26% rate applies. However, if your net AMTI is over $175,000, the rate is 28%.

As an auditee, you pay the *higher* of the two taxes: regular tax or AMT. You don't pay both. At this point, you have little choice. Your "tax die" is cast.

12

CLOSING MATTERS

An Auditor Is Required To Submit To You A Written Report Itemizing His Examination Changes. His "Explanation Of Adjustments" Is Stereotyped And Disconnected From The Actual Events At Audit. Nevertheless, His Change Report Starts The Administrative Sequence For Closing The Audit. In Some Cases, REPETITIVE AUDITS May Be Involved. If (Within 30 Days) You Do Not Agree With The Report, You Can Seek A "Revised Report," Or Request A Hearing Before An IRS Appeals Officer. At Any Point Along The Way, You Can Consent And Pay The Additional Tax, Plus Penalties And Interest.

Sooner or later, every audit must come to an end. This is the point at which the issues raised have been considered, reconsidered, and rehashed; neither side can muster new facts or positions to allow or disallow the items claimed. It is that point at which the auditee and auditor each knows where the other stands. The ending of an audit is not an agreement per se, but is merely a point of reference in administrative time.

The timespan between the beginning of an audit and ending it varies considerably. Much depends on the issues involved, the scheduling of appointments between auditee and auditor, the attitude and preparedness of the auditee, the attitude and reasonableness of the auditor, and the "chemistry" between the two.

In most cases, the IRS prefers to close an audit within three years of the due date for filing a return (Sec. 6501(a)). Most audits do not start until 18 months after the return due date. Consequently, this means approximately 18 months between beginning an audit and closing it.

It is possible to extend an audit beyond the three-year date. This can be done by mutual consent between auditee and auditor. To do so, a special form is required, namely: Form 872—*Consent to Extend Time to Assess Tax*. The extension may be for any length of time necessary for closing the audit.

Closing an audit does not mean that a taxpayer/auditee is deprived of all rights of protest or appeal. It merely means that the audit issues will be summarized, and that the proposed adjustments, if any, will be made in writing. The closing forms will be prepared by the auditor. He must give the auditee a copy of his prepared forms. There is space on the forms for the auditee to agree with the auditor, if he so chooses.

Pre-Closing Review

During the course of an examination, an auditor will make numerous informal notes. These notes are made on tablets of paper of no particular format. The notes include factual information, rough computations, and notations by the auditor to himself. The notes are handwritten and highly preliminary. They constitute the auditor's "working papers."

Most auditors will subhead their working papers with the same nomenclature of the issues raised in the audit notification letter that started the audit. The sequence of the issues examined generally follows the preference of the auditee. Most auditors will "give a little" on the examination sequence so long as the auditee is acting in good faith and is organized in his presentation of his supporting documentation.

An auditor's working papers are not the final say. They are merely his preliminary "lining up of your ducks" for shooting down if he can. Do not hassle the auditor on every handwritten note, symbol, scratch mark, or figure that he enters on his work papers. Concentrate on supporting your own position with factual documentation; do not concern yourself with the auditor's note taking. He has to cover certain procedural points to satisfy his group supervisor and his department manager.

As the examination nears its end, the auditor will become more systematic in his notes. For reporting to his superiors, he will start to summarize matters, usually, on a separate sheet. He will organize his notes into columns, such as:

1. Item at issue   (general classification)
2. Amount shown   (as claimed by auditee)
3. Corrected amount   (as determined by auditor)
4. Adjustment   (increase or decrease)

When an auditor starts summarizing his notes, you know that he is approaching making up his mind. When you sense this, or when you have provided all of the justification and verification that you possibly can, say to him:

I would like to review matters and see where we stand at this point. If I have missed some things, I may be able to get further documentation or statements for you.

The principal role of an auditor is that of *verifier of facts*. The facts, of course, are the entries you made on your tax return. The more black-and-white you can establish your facts and position, the less likely he is to show an adjustment figure in his summary columns. An auditor is not a judge of facts nor an interpreter of law. However, most auditors will allow some persuasive pitches by an auditee where different implications of the facts prevail. Because the "burden of proof" is on your shoulders, you have the right to make persuasive efforts, where applicable, to clinch the verifications. The point here is to get your last licks in before the auditor's mind firms.

When the auditor reviews his summary position with you, do not try to argue or continue the persuasion. He has a time schedule to meet, and he has a written report to make. So let him tell you his position, and *you* make the notes. This will give you a preview of what his proposed changes will be. This also will enable you to prejudge whether you are on the winning side or losing side of the audit.

Change Reports

Any changes that an auditor may have in mind must be presented to you in writing. Not his working papers, mind you, but on official IRS forms. Rarely will an auditor prepare these forms while you sit and wait. He much prefers to mail them to you. The mailing

IRS	REPORT OF INDIVIDUAL INCOME TAX EXAMINATION CHANGES		Dept. of Treasury

Name / Address of Auditee	Audit Year	Filing Status	Audit Group
	Date of Report	Identifying Number	IRS District

INCOME AND DEDUCTION AMOUNTS ADJUSTED			
Ref. No.	Item Changed	Amount Shown	Corrected Amount	Increase (Decrease)

TOTAL ADJUSTMENTS: INCREASE (DECREASE) ⟶ ☐

TAX COMPUTATIONS

TAX CREDITS

OTHER TAXES

CORRECTED TAX ⟶ ☐

DEFICIENCY (Increase in tax)

OVERASSESSMENT (Decrease in tax)

PREPAYMENTS

BALANCE DUE ⟶ ☐

REFUND ┈┈▶ ☐

PENALTIES ⟶ ☐

Auditee's Consent and Signature Block

Fig. 12.1 - Edited Format of Nonbusiness Audit Report

will include a preprinted transmittal letter . . . and tons of computer printout sheets.

Basically, there are two types of examination change reports. There is a nonbusiness audit report and, separately, a business audit report. The nonbusiness report is for individuals whose primary sources of income are from salaries, wages, pensions, passive investments, and the like. The business report is for individuals whose primary source of income is from self-employment or from a trade or business in which the auditee is a participating owner. Because of these occupational differences, different report forms are used for each type of audit.

For nonbusiness audits, the auditor prepares: *Report of Individual Income Tax Examination Changes*. A subheading on this form reads: "Income and Deduction Amounts Adjusted." There is one such report for each year under audit. The general arrangement of a nonbusiness audit report is presented in Figure 12.1. The report is dated but is not signed by the auditor.

For business audits, the auditor prepares: *Report of Income Tax Examination Changes*. The word "individual" is missing because this form is used also for partnerships and corporations. A subheading on this form reads: "Adjustments to Income." The form is similar to that in Figure 12.1 except that it covers *three* years: the audit year, its preceding year, and its succeeding year. This is because in most business audits there are items such as depreciation, inventory, expenses, credits, carrybacks, and carryforwards which dovetail from adjacent years into the audit year. The form is dated and signed by the "examining officer" (auditor).

Attached to either change report are (alleged) explanations of the adjustments. These explanations are supposed to provide the authoritative basis upon which the auditor relies. Most of the explanations are stereotyped and uninformative.

Near the bottom line of either form is a *deficiency* (increase in tax, meaning "balance due") or an *overassessment* (decrease in tax, meaning "refund due"). If there is additional tax to pay, the actual bottom line will also include *penalties*. The penalties are assertive and automatic.

Read the Covering Letter

Whichever change form you receive will be accompanied by a covering letter. This letter consists of two sheets of paper computer-printed on one side. It is "signed" on the second sheet with a facsimile signature of the IRS District Director to whom the auditor reports.

Do not take lightly this covering letter. It starts the clock running for administrative closing procedures. The letter is dated.

The date is recorded on the master case load schedule maintained by the district audit chief.

Many — too many — auditee recipients tend to skim this covering letter and set it aside. This is a grave mistake. You must read it carefully, as you have a 30-day time constraint.

The letter starts out quite courteously. The first paragraph says—

Enclosed are two copies of our report explaining why we believe adjustments should be made in the amount of your tax. Please look this report over and let us know whether you agree with our findings.

The second paragraph tells you what to do if you accept the findings as is. You simply sign, pay the additional tax, or allow them to bill you . . . with interest.

The third paragraph tells you what to do if you do *not* accept their findings. This paragraph says—

If you do not accept our findings, you have 30 days from the date of this letter to do one of the following:
1. Mail us any additional evidence or information you would like us to consider.
2. Request a discussion of our findings with one of our examiners. At that time you may submit additional evidence or information you would like us to consider. If you plan to come in for a discussion, please phone or write us in advance so that we can arrange a convenient time and place.

If you do nothing within 30 days, your case will go automatically into administrative closing. Trying to restore your rights after 30 days is a rough road to hoe. You are in administrative default. You will receive a "statutory notice of deficiency" which allows you 90 days to petition the U.S. Tax Court. Otherwise, you will be billed for the additional tax . . . plus penalties . . . plus interest.

In a business audit report, the third paragraph of the covering letter is more formal. Its tone is one of "shoving it down your throat." Accept or go to Appeals. The specific wording is—

If you do not accept our findings, you may request a conference with our Office of Regional Director of Appeals. Most cases *considered at that level are settled satisfactorily. . . . If the proposed increase or decrease in tax is more than $2,500, please submit a written protest. . . . You will be contacted so that an appointment can be scheduled with Appeals.*

We suggest that you not accept any auditor's "findings" the first time around. There must be some substantiating matters that you overlooked. Almost any auditee can come up with some kind of additional evidence or information. So, give it a try. But, before you do, read the "explanations."

Example Explanations

One of the universal complaints against the IRS is the general arrogance with which it explains its actions and behavior. This arrogance spills over into every auditor's report. Although there is an attachment labeled: *Explanation of Adjustments*, the so-called "explanations" are stereotyped, preprogrammed computer bits. They are disconnected from the actual events that took place at audit.

To give you the flavor involved, we are citing below five specific examples of the type of official explanations in an audit-change report. The examples are not fictitious in any way. They are lifted directly from recent audit reports. The adjustment amounts are shown in dollars.

Item: Employee Business Expenses

Since you did not establish that the business expense shown on your tax return was paid or incurred during the taxable year and that the expense was ordinary and necessary to your own business, we have disallowed the amount shown $2,926

Item: Charitable Contributions

The amount shown on your return as a deduction for charitable contributions is not allowable in full because it has not been established that the total amount was paid during the tax year or that the items met the requirements of section 170 of the Internal Revenue Code. Accordingly, your taxable income is increased $9,031

Item: Schedule C Supplies

We have disallowed the amount shown on your return because you did not furnish information needed to support the claimed deduction *$12,341*

Item: Schedule F Expenses

With the information provided, we have no alternative but to treat this as a business engaged in not-for-profit. Under the Internal Revenue Code rules, a business must show a profit in 3 of 5 consecutive years. However, we did allow your expenses up to your gross income, as these are allowable under the code. The 3-year total adjustment is *$16,533*

Item: Negligence Penalty

It has been determined that the underpayment of tax is due to negligence or intentional disregard of rules and regulations. Consequently, an addition to the tax is charged as provided by Section 6662(a) of the Internal Revenue Code. The amount of addition to tax due to negligence is *$5,058*

If you are satisfied with the type of explanations above with respect to your audit, sign (and date) the report form at the bottom, and return it to the auditor in the envelope provided. Pay the additional tax . . . and penalty. You'll be billed later for the interest.

Give It One Good Try

You may be, but we're not, satisfied with the types of explanations above. They should be more connected. They should cite specifically what took place at the audit, and why a particular document or amount was not acceptable. They should also indicate what would be acceptable in alternative form.

In true reality, the explanations (so-called), and the District Director's covering letter transmitting them, are nothing more than legal sops. The auditor and his or her supervisor have no intention of changing their changes. They have a group performance quota to meet, and that's what they are going to do.

As a result, taxpayers often complain to their Congressman (or Congresswoman) about the IRS's auditing practices. The

Congressperson contacts your local District Director, who is an unelected bureaucrat. Because he is unelected, he tends to be snobbish towards Congresspersons. The District Director gets out the covering letter and the file copy of the audit change report. He then tells the Congressperson how the IRS is "upholding the law." The District Director also tells the Congressperson that the taxpayer was given an opportunity to submit additional information, but that he or she declined.

To take some of the wind out of the IRS's chest beating, we think you should give at least one good try at changing the audit report. First, do your homework. Then prepare a written **Request for Reconsideration**. Address it to the auditor and send it Certified Mail. Print in the white space at the heading: SAVE THIS DOCUMENT IN CASE OF APPEAL.

To exemplify what we mean, glance back at the $16,533 item above regarding Schedule F (Farm) expenses. The auditee (a woman) had a college degree in animal husbandry. She bought 50 head of cows and 2 registered bulls, to start a cattle feeding and breeding business. The auditor was flippant and nonchalant, and gung-ho on the not-for-profit presumptions of Section 183. This miffed the auditee to the point where she decided to do something about it. This, in part, is what she wrote to the auditor:

> *You have erred in the interpretation and application of Code Sec. 183. You have made a subjective inference rather than an objective analysis of all facts and circumstances. Sec. 183 applies only to . . . those activities which are carried on primarily as a sport, hobby, or for recreation. [Reg. 1.183-2(a).] There is no sport, hobby, or recreational aspect whatsoever to the branding, feeding, calving, vaccination, culling, gathering up dead carcasses, and shoveling manure for 50 head of commercial cattle and their calves. These are not house pets and they cannot be raced for sport or ridden for pleasure. You have considered net losses only . . . and no other factors.*
>
> *Pursuant to Reg. 1.183-2(b), the specific factors on which you have erred are as follows:*
> *(1) . . . [through] . . . (9).*

Some seven months after the letter was sent, the auditee received a form response from the District Director. The form said:

*We are pleased to tell you that our examination of your tax returns for the above period(s) shows **no change is necessary** in your reported tax.* [Emphasis added.]

This is called a "No Change" audit letter. Very few of these IRS letters are sent out. The reason: most auditees don't try for reconsideration. Shouldn't you try?

Repetitive Audits

No matter what we've said previously, every audit is an inconvenience and a hassle. One's first audit or two can be instructive in learning what our income tax system is all about. But if you get "selected" for audit year after year . . . after year, it gets to be a real pain. You inevitably ask yourself: "Why is the IRS so stupid?" Especially if repetitive audit issues are similar and the adjustments are minor (order of 5% or less of tax shown on your original return).

We know first-hand of numerous cases where certain taxpayers are audited again and again. This is because the selections are based on "DIF profiles" (recall Chapter 2) which, for some occupations, repeat themselves yearly. For illustration purposes, we'll cite three cases where taxpayers have been audited between five and seven times in the 10-year period 1985 through 1995.

In Case A, the taxpayer was a sales representative who traveled a lot for various show manufacturers. He was audited **seven** times. All resulted in zero or negligible adjustments. Two weeks after his 7th audit, he received a "No Change" letter. The next day, he committed suicide! THIS IS A TRUE CASE.

In Case B, the taxpayer was a language translator who engaged about 60 freelance translators of all languages. She was audited five times. After the 5th audit (and receiving a "No Change" letter for the third time), she changed from a proprietorship to a corporation, hoping that would change her DIF profile.

In Case C, the taxpayer was an animal pharmacist, selling food supplements and antibiotics to poultry farmers, cattlemen, and hog ranchers in 10 western states of the U.S. and Canada. He had his own private airplane and flew to his customers regularly. He was audited six times. Every audit resulted in some adjustments: two were refunds, four were deficiencies. The average net revenue to the government was $30 per hour of IRS audit time. This is very poor cost effectiveness for a process where the performance quota is set at between $300 and $500 per hour.

The IRS claims that it will discontiue an audit, if you are subjected to a repetitive selection within a two-year period. In reality, the IRS will not always honor its claim when its "case load" requires that its auditors be kept busy. The sole purpose of auditing is to generate more revenue. Perhaps the IRS figures that if it audits the same taxpayer often enough it may stumble into a revenue bonanza.

To, or Not to, Appeal

Every auditee has — or should have — his own tolerance level for additional tax he will pay or not pay. If the total due is less than $100, many auditees will simply pay it and go on to other matters. If the amount is over $1,000, many will fight it. Each person has to set his own additional tax tolerance and proceed accordingly. The simplest procedure, if you want to contest the auditor's "findings," is to appeal within the IRS itself.

The audit adjustments covering letter contains a paragraph which reads (in part)—

If you do not accept our findings . . . call us at the telephone number above within 30 days . . . to request a conference with an Appeals Officer. You must provide all pertinent documentation and facts concerning disputed issues to the examiner [auditor] *before your case is forwarded to the Appeals Office.*

Now, you have a decision to make. Do you appeal, or do you not appeal? An appeal can be instructive — and may even be helpful — but it also can be time consuming. Invariably, you will be asked to sign Form 872: Consent to Extend Time to Assess Tax.

There are many valid reasons for an audit appeal. Among these reasons are:

1. An overzealous auditor who has misread the intent of the applicable tax code section, and has harped only on the letter of the law.
2. A hard-nosed auditor who will not listen to reason, and who has rejected your substantiation on opinionated or frivolous grounds.

3. A prime issue that really should not be a prime issue, except for the fact that the IRS position is academic, unrealistic, and bureaucracy-building.
4. When the facts presented at audit can lead to two or more interpretations, but the auditor chose that interpretation most favorable to the government.
5. Where existing applicable law is silent or unclear on a tax point, and you can argue plausibly under another code section that gives you approximately the results you desire.

In the appeals process, you must stick to the audit issues changed. You cannot veer off onto new issues, or seek the allowance of a deduction that was not raised in the audit. An appeal is strictly a "second attempt" to reduce your additional tax payment.

Appeals are handled by an entirely separate division of the Internal Revenue Service. If you appeal, your case has to be carefully packaged for new eyes to see. The auditor's working papers have to be cleaned up; your position has to be summarized by the auditor; the initial and revised reports have to be submitted; and a formal statement of position by the Examination Division has to be prepared. It is as though the case were going from one federal bureaucracy (Audit) to another federal bureaucracy (Appeals). Additional time and new personalities become involved.

Usually, going to appeals requires considerable research on the applicable tax code sections involved. It also requires a review of prior Tax Court decisions that might have a bearing on your case. Discussion of the appeals process and the "winning" thereof is beyond the scope herein.

At this point, we must assume that you are not going to appeal. That is, you will accept the revised report as submitted. How do you go about making this acceptance?

Answer: The second sentence in the audit report says—

*If you accept our findings, please sign the **consent to assessment and collection** portion at the bottom of the report . . . within 30 days. If additional tax is due, you may want to pay it now to limit the interest charge; otherwise, we will bill you.* [Emphasis added.]

Billing time runs anywhere from 90 to 180 days or more after your signature. When you do receive the final bill it will say: PAY THIS AMOUNT $_____. You have exactly 10 days in which to do so . . . or else. The "or else" is that they can levy upon your wages, bank, savings, and/or investment accounts and *seize* the amount due. The seized amount will include further interest, penalties, and charges.

Unless you purposely want the educational experience of a tax seizure, you might as well pay the additional tax and interest at the time you sign the audit report. If you sign and pay at the same time, your case is essentially closed . . . for that audit year.

Post-Audit Critique

There is no recorded evidence that legislation ever has been introduced in Congress, or is being introduced, or ever will be introduced to eliminate income and other taxes in America. The income tax laws got started in earnest in 1913. From that time on, the laws, regulations, and rules have grown more exacting and more sophisticated, year after year. Income taxation is big business to Big Government. The audit process will never go away.

You should regard your audit as a unique educational experience. It encompasses the kind of instruction that can never be taught in our great halls of academic learning. You see your government and yourself pitted against each other, in an arena in which you are entirely on your own. This is your opportunity for becoming a better citizen, a better voter, and a better taxpayer.

For one thing, your audit should have taught you to assess your own character, persistence, and determination to win. Although time consuming and, perhaps, nerve wracking, the experience should have increased your self-respect and self-confidence. You need this to take on future audits, if and when your return is again selected.

Conversely, the audit may have increased your disrespect for the IRS (and for government). Although the auditor himself/herself may have been cordial and reasonable, he/she was applying rules which, as you may have observed on your own, are one-sided: the government's side.

The rationale for this one-sidedness derives from the politico-legal philosophy of "protecting the revenue" of government. Those who espouse this philosophy are one of the following: on the government payroll, participate in government entitlements, benefit from special-interest contracts, or are in the legal/accounting system benefiting from the tax laws enacted.

Most auditees make one common post-audit mistake. They are so glad to get the audit over with that they triumphantly toss away all of their audit papers. "I never want to go through that again," they say to themselves.

What a mistake! In this era of electronic surveillance and computer tyranny, what makes you think you are exempt from senseless, repetitive audits? The repetitive audit cases we cited a few pages earlier are true. Any day, you could be a victim of audit harassment.

So, don't throw away your audit papers: the examination notice, the audit change (or no-change) report, and all correspondence between you and the IRS for the audit year(s). Organize these papers chronologically and put them in a separate file of their own. Review them from time to time.

From your audit experience(s), you should develop future tax goals. In targeting these goals, you should say to yourself:

If I am audited again, I will prove that they are wasting their time. Furthermore, every time they audit me, in one way or another, I will derive new expertise for greater tax savings.

This kind of determination becomes the privilege and power that develops from an audit. Whether you win, lose, or draw, completing an audit can be a confidence-building experience. Glean all that you can from this experience.

ABOUT
THE AUTHOR

Holmes F. Crouch

Born on a small farm in southern Maryland, Holmes was graduated from the U.S. Coast Guard Academy with a Bachelor's Degree in Marine Engineering. While serving on active duty, he wrote many technical articles on maritime matters. After attaining the rank of Lieutenant Commander, he resigned to pursue a career as a nuclear engineer.

Continuing his education, he earned a Master's Degree in Nuclear Engineering from the University of California. He also authored two books on nuclear propulsion. As a result of the tax write-offs associated with writing these books, the IRS audited his returns. The IRS's handling of the audit procedure so annoyed Holmes that he undertook to become as knowledgeable as possible regarding tax procedures. He became a licensed private Tax Practitioner by passing an examination administered by the IRS. Having attained this credential, he started his own tax preparation and counseling business in 1972.

In the early years of his tax practice, he was a regular talk-show guest on San Francisco's KGO Radio responding to hundreds of phone-in tax questions from listeners. He was a much sought-after guest speaker at many business seminars and taxpayer meetings. He also provided counseling on special tax problems, such as divorce matters, property exchanges, timber harvesting, mining ventures, animal breeding, independent contractors, selling businesses, and offices-at-home. Over the past 25 years, he has prepared nearly 10,000 tax returns for individuals, estates, trusts, and small businesses (in partnership and corporate form).

During the tax season of January through April, he prepares returns in a unique manner. During a single meeting, he completes the return . . . *on the spot!* The client leaves with his return signed, sealed, and in a stamped envelope. His unique approach to preparing returns and his personal interest in his clients' tax affairs have honed his professional proficiency. His expertise extends through itemized deductions, computer-matching of income sources, capital gains and losses, business expenses and cost of goods, residential rental expenses, limited and general partnership activities, closely-held corporations, to family farms and ranches.

He remembers spending 12 straight hours completing a doctor's complex return. The next year, the doctor, having moved away, utilized a large accounting firm to prepare his return. Their accountant was so impressed by the manner in which the prior return was prepared that he recommended the doctor travel the 500 miles each year to have Holmes continue doing it.

He recalls preparing a return for an unemployed welder, for which he charged no fee. Two years later the welder came back and had his return prepared. He paid the regular fee . . . and then added a $300 tip.

During the off season, he represents clients at IRS audits and appeals. In one case a shoe salesman's audit was scheduled to last three hours. However, after examining Holmes' documentation it was concluded in 15 minutes with "no change" to his return. In another instance he went to an audit of a custom jeweler that the IRS dragged out for more than six hours. But, supported by Holmes' documentation, the client's return was accepted by the IRS with "no change."

Then there was the audit of a language translator that lasted two full days. The auditor scrutinized more than $1.25 million in gross receipts, all direct costs, and operating expenses. Even though all expensed items were documented and verified, the auditor decided that more than $23,000 of expenses ought to be listed as capital items for depreciation instead. If this had been enforced it would have resulted in a significant additional amount of tax. Holmes strongly disagreed and after many hours explanation got the amount reduced by more than 60% on behalf of his client.

He has dealt extensively with gift, death and trust tax returns. These preparations have involved him in the tax aspects of wills, estate planning, trustee duties, probate, marital and charitable bequests, gift and death exemptions, and property titling.

Although not an attorney, he prepares Petitions to the U.S. Tax Court for clients. He details the IRS errors and taxpayer facts by citing pertinent sections of tax law and regulations. In a recent case involving an attorney's ex-spouse, the IRS asserted a tax deficiency of $155,000. On behalf of his client, he petitioned the Tax Court and within six months the IRS conceded the case.

Over the years, Holmes has observed that the IRS is not the industrious, impartial, and competent federal agency that its official public imaging would have us believe.

He found that, at times, under the slightest pretext, the IRS has interpreted against a taxpayer in order to assess maximum penalties, and may even delay pending matters so as to increase interest due on additional taxes. He has confronted the IRS in his own behalf on five separate occasions, going before the U.S. Claims Court, U.S. District Court, and U.S. Tax Court. These were court actions that tested specific sections of the Internal Revenue Code which he found ambiguous, inequitable, and abusively interpreted by the IRS.

Disturbed by the conduct of the IRS and by the general lack of tax knowledge by most individuals, he began an innovative series of taxpayer-oriented Federal tax guides. To fulfill this need, he undertook the writing of a series of guidebooks that provide in-depth knowledge on one tax subject at a time. He focuses on subjects that plague taxpayers all throughout the year. Hence, his formulation of the "Allyear" Tax Guide series.

The author is indebted to his wife, Irma Jean, and daughter, Barbara MacRae, for the word processing and computer graphics that turn his experiences into the reality of these publications. Holmes welcomes comments, questions, and suggestions from his readers. He can be contacted in California at (408) 867-2628, or by writing to the publisher's address.

ALLYEAR Tax Guides
by Holmes F. Crouch

All of the above available at bookstores, libraries, and on the internet

For a free 8-page catalog,
or information about the above titles, contact:
ALLYEAR Tax Guides
20484 Glen Brae Drive, Saratoga, CA 95070
Phone: (408) 867-2628   Fax: (408) 867-6466